ABANDONED QUARRY

MERCER
UNIVERSITY PRESS

Endowed by
TOM WATSON BROWN
and
THE WATSON-BROWN FOUNDATION, INC.

Abandoned Quarry

New and Selected Poems

JOHN LANE

MERCER UNIVERSITY PRESS
MACON, GEORGIA

MUP/P428

© 2010 Mercer University Press
1400 Coleman Avenue
Macon, Georgia 31207

First Edition.

Books published by Mercer University Press are printed on acid free
paper that meets the requirements of American National Standard for
Information Sciences—Permanence of Paper for Printed Library
Materials.

Mercer University Press is a member of Green Press initiative
(greenpressinitiative.org), a nonprofit organization working to help
publishers and printers increase their use of recycled paper and decrease
their use of fiber derived from endangered forests. This book is printed
on recycled paper.

978-0-88146-241-8

Lane, John, 1954-
Abandoned quarry : new and selected poems / John Lane. -- 1st ed
p. cm.
ISBN 978-0-88146-241-8 (pbk. : alk. paper)
I. Title.
PS3562.A48442A23 2011
811'.54--dc22
2011002065

ACKNOWLEDGMENTS

Poems reprinted here first appeared in *Blair and Ketchum's Country Journal, The Chattahoochee Review, Columbia: A Magazine of Poetry and Prose, The Davidson Miscellany, Harvard Magazine, House Organ, Illuminations, Interim, Ironwood, ISLE, Literary Bird Journal, Loblolly, The New Review, Nexus, The Northstone Review, Ploughshares, Poetry Northwest, Point Magazine, The Asheville Poetry Review, The New Virginia Review, South Carolina Review, Skyline, Snake Nation Review, Stone Country, South Florida Poetry Review, Tar River Poetry Review, Town Creek Poetry, Virginia Quarterly Review.*

Poems also appeared in these pamphlets, chapbooks, and collections:

Thin Creek (Copper Canyon Press, 1978)
Quarries (Briarpatch Press, 1984)
As the World Around Us Sleeps (Briarpatch Press, 1991)
Body Poems (New Native Press, 1991)
Against Information & Other Poems (New Native Press, 1995)
The Dead Father Poems (Horse & Buggy/Holocene, 1999)
Noble Trees (Hub City Writers Project, 2003)

"Seeing Wild Horses" was reprinted in the *1984 Anthology of Magazine Verse and Yearbook of American Poetry* (Beverly Hills: Monitor Book Company, 1984).

Four poems, written in collaboration with Nashville fiddler Mark O'Connor, appeared as liner notes in O'Connor's Sony Classical release, *Midnight on the Water*, April 1998. Four of the tracks take their titles from the poems.

"Hounds Chasing Deer in the Suburbs" first appeared in *Elemental South*, a collection of Southern nature writing, edited by Dorinda Dalmeyer (Athens & London: The University of Georgia Press, 2004)

"High Meadow Poem" first appeared in a *Millennial Sampler of South Carolina Poetry* edited by Gilbert Allen and William C. Rogers (Greenville SC: Ninety-Six Press, 2005)

The author wishes to thank the National Endowment of the Arts, the South Carolina Arts Commission, the Henry Hoyns Endowment at the University of Virginia, and Wofford College for grants and fellowships during which many of these poems were written, the staff of Mercer University Press, and Philip Lee Williams. And special thanks to Sebastian Matthews for help with the order of the book.

For David Romtvedt

CONTENTS

I. *Thin Creek* (1978)

THIN CREEK

But who could be coming? And from where?
She lingers by the railing,
green flesh, green hair,
dreaming of the bitter sea.
                    —Federico Garcia Lorca

Mountains muscle early sun back.
Fog grips low places, creek bottoms
and laurel draws. I wait on the ridge.
Below, in the steep yard, your father
up early, rips summer's green vines
from long step-rails.

Honeysuckle, wild rose, Virginia creeper
clinch-wood rails with flat, stiff veins.
Sweat darkens his old dress shirt,
and fists of steam rise from his back.

Inside, you and your sisters sleep
until dreams crack you awake.
They fill the room, someone moves
below in the kitchen.

A fire grows beside the mountain street,
The burning vines spit and hiss.
Your father lugs a thick pile, paces
below me in a silence that smoothes
sleeping houses like a chant.

You dress quickly. The slap of backdoor
against frame tears through mountain air.
Your father stops. His shadow
rocks scorched ground in front of him.

You pull me up the banks of Thin Creek,
through green shade, dry cedar smell,
dark leaves of hemlock.
In the oaks and poplars, you open
your clothes to my cool hands.

Sun finds the hillside, morning
cold climbs out.
The hill slope sweats under us,
sky cracks from its sudden stiffness.
Ants crawl thrown-off clothes like men
looking for someone lost.

Above us smoke from your father's fire
enters the trees on a thin arm of dark air.

II. from *QUARRIES* (1984)

QUARRIES

Even as a boy I begged to be drunk
on immense stretches of emptiness—
the earth laid open, gutted, then
stripped of its hard belly of stone.
You could not keep me from the ragged edge,
the eroding lip, the dry drop defining
the limits of blast and cutters' craft.

I thirsted for losses in the world
outside myself, and squatted at edges
of quarries to watch stone cutters
work in their depths and distances.
Like slaves of the stone itself,
they cabled the coarse tongues
of granite to the gargling dozers.

I watched them work within the gray cloud,
and longed to stand with thick dust
stirring, then settling slowly around me.
I longed to grow into a man and work
to quarry the emptiness outward
until all was level again.

BETHESDA ROAD

Years ago I wandered here as a boy,
lonely among hardwoods, sifting nearby
creek gravel for bird points, pottery.
Now the moon tightens on this outcrop
of soapstone, stemmed where bowls
were chipped loose, fell clean of rock,
in another darkness, 5,000 years ago.
I click on my flashlight, the stone
clutter is everywhere.
Wildflowers push through broken bowls
at my feet—Queen Anne's lace,
here at the edge of the fields,
chicory, tight buds in the night—
like the worked stone itself flowers.
Below, in the remaining hardwood groves
shadows sink in the trunks of oaks.

A possum prowls thick rows
of pines near the ridge of the next hill.
Then, stopped in my flashlight beam
it haunches up in a small country of trees.
I click off the light and the possum,
given night back like a room
to enter, scuttles through the pines.
I follow into its darkness.

For miles I hear the song
of its feet through dry pine,
cut-over fields, a last still stream,
into the first tentative lights of houses.
Then finally I stand at the edge of yards
and listen as the possum rifles cans—
this night and all it accommodates
its only vision, and mine,
as the world around us sleeps.

THANKSGIVING, 1968

We are amid fallow fields,
Herbert, or no, we have walked
to the tree line and into
the thinning woods.

There is frost
or maybe the world is frozen.

I pause where a leaf is a pane
of glass, crack it with
my new shotgun's butt.
Damp ground opens underneath.

I think my breath is the man
squatting beside me
but he rises and walks ahead
through the trees with a gun.
It is you, and my breath
is only a child I trail
behind when I follow.

The first shot kicks hardest.
The gun bites air,
then shatters, out-fall
bits of fur, small teeth,
and the sun as if
it was hiding there.

WAKING IN THE BLUE RIDGE

In the animal light of early morning
dreams persist but I am quickly
victim to the world's precision—

how oaks become one
in a web of blue above,
and the fox bursts
toward the nested quail,
or in tricks of color
copperheads coil
where they could not be.

All this in the hour
before breakfast, in the heaven
of unnoticed verdancy and light.

THE RIVER FALLING

Once, we slept in oak woods,
zipped our two bags together, pulled free
of flannel shirts, shucked jeans,
counted the sad light of planes
flying to Asheville until the darkness
of dying oak leaves offered up some light.
All night Bradley Falls argued the moon down.

That morning, we climbed down,
took off our clothes, listened
to a song of water leveling with stone.
You sat in a hole where the river once
licked its own bed. I squatted, pressed silt
in my palms, caught round stones dragging
the creek bottom. The fall sun was up,
cliff-high, a star in a stub oak.

I squinted, spoke,
"You know I could be this river, easily
live my life between two places, two women."

You watched the falls, the perfect sadness
of the river falling. I swear the wet air
hummed, water dug for something to hold.
You turned, said,
"Then go, the seed's in us all, this leaving."

AT CHEROKEE FORD, SOUTH CAROLINA

Above the Broad River, a hawk
sleeps in the wind, then banks
and wakes, looking for snakes
or rabbits out in the heat.
Power lines wading the shallows

on treated pine poles could
be Whitman's cavalry crossing
the ford, or only the complex
of light and color attracting
the hawk's yellow tilted eye.
Unlike the hawk, I am caught

by a purely human equation:
to balance what the creature sees
with my apparition of the past
and the line's transgression
of gullied landscape, to find
a point of rest within the three—

but now, out of time, small eddies
of light still catch the hawk's eye.

TOM'S FARM

ONE
Bessie sweeps her part of the yard.
She always said bare earth is better than grass,
the devil being real and living in snakes.
Every summer Sunday she leads hope home
on a leash, walking slow.

She stares up from sleep under an oak.
I say "Sleep's better than church, Bessie."
She says, "You sleep on Sundays, son,
you never know how that church does sing."

I laugh, stand and stretch.
She smiles, walks on toward home,
her Sunday skirts swishing the air.
She's singing, then she's gone.

TWO
Today we chased the last sunning
black snake from Bessie's yard.
The abandoned farm fields of South Carolina
are brown with the cold again.
A red sun settles in the limbs
of a thin woods. Even the pines
dull this time of year.

The pigs are nearly grown. We'll slaughter
soon after October's first freeze.

In the evening the cows along Stillhouse Road
follow each other home.

THREE
Winter snapped shut with the rhythm
of work: bush-axe, slingblade, maul.
Clearing the pondsite of brush
my wet boots froze.

On gray work like that
my body burned for days.

The garden plot is stiff with frost.
Bessie turns to her winter chores.
I hear her axe strike in early morning.

Now, alone in my room,
the late afternoon settles in quiet.
Coffee steams from the stove.
Outside, a few leaves listen,
waiting for the first snow.

THE HOMECOMING OF OSCEOLA

Edisto Island, South Carolina

Fifty miles south of Charleston,
south of the cell at Fort Moultrie
where he once dreamed the long hours
through sticky heat and silences.
I walk the last high tide of the day
to find bones of glacial South Carolina
washed up from black marshes.

I recite particulars of that gone world:
glyptodont, mastodon, bison, dugong.
Their fragments rattle my pockets.
Wind skitters along tops of waves,
up dunes, to the estuarine glint
beyond. An incoming tide measures
marsh grass, making a low sound
like someone sighing.

       ★

From a hammock deep in *Pa-hay-okee*
he listened as flat-bottomed boats
of the US Navy slid through thick
saw grass and mosquitoes.

"We will flush him like a rat
from his savage hole,"
an Army captain mumbled to a slow fire
of dry thatch-palm and torchwood,

to ten men, snake-scared and malarial,
who dreamed of Baltimore and Richmond.

They listened too,
and the Seminole War dragged on.

*

Ivory from the tusk of mammoth,
tooth of *Equus,* tooth of *Bison bison,*
dugong ribs, cracked leg bones of *Ursus.*

*

Last winter, walking here at Edisto
I dug half a skullcap from the tidal sand—
the frontal bone, eye-ridges intact.
The bleached whole of it brown
from tannin stain, buried years
under water of cypress swamps.
I placed it over my ear—
wanting a song in the dead
long months before spring—
that curve of bone
held a soft roar,
like a tightly cupped hand
or the dull slap of sea
on a turtle-haunted shore
or a winter wind rattling
dry palmetto fronds gathered for kindling.

*

Osceola finally rooted out, brought to
South Carolina.

Seminole, "Men-who-go-free,"
of the five tribes of the Creek, of the Piedmont
and mountains.

The guard spat in standing water,
leaned on a sweating stone wall
next to windowless cell.

Inside, Osceola's last chant
rose from the cot, from the stoneware mug,
pried the stones with sound—
his window to the next world.

⋆

I walk up the receding beach,
past peeling wood rails of empty cottages,
through low thick brush and live oak
to reach the back of the island,
where St. Pierre Creek eats
at the Indian mound.

⋆

The guard listened:

spittle spread on the water,
a soul reentering a body

⋆

A mound of midden
arches flat coastal country.
It would take twenty years to grub
this many shellfish from the tidal creeks.
I still smell the oysters and clams steaming
in salt and fresh oak, or eaten raw
and piled here 4,000 years ago.
A lone buck is spooked
in dry leaves by my hard boots.
I look out over a marsh the color of shale.
It is that moment just before the tide
shifts, or right after.
The empty shells hiss.

⋆

"And you who keep me here
know nothing about cages."

The coast is quiet.
A creek turns over in its sleep.

TO A GEOLOGIST

For John Harrington

I've been reading Blake and thought
of you—"To see a World
in a grain of sand." I know
what follows, Eternity, but for me,
here, time catches.

Summers when Discovery Bay
clears birds drift in.
Gulls, mallards, coots, even once
a lone, Arctic loon.
In the evening they float on darkening water,
bending wings, riffling feathers,
last light a bright dream in small brains.

I remember a geology lab
when a busload of football players
and English majors stood on a mountain
road in the Blue Ridge and boomed out
in sheer joy, with a child's fascination,
your chant to the Mountain King—
praising a mudslide on a nearby highway.
You, the troubadour of soil-creep
and erosion.

Now you write you're starting
a novel about death, that leveler.
You say we two are much alike,
and not to forsake the keen eye
of the geologist.

John, I want you to know, here,
across all the distances of this continent,
glaciers are working mountains down.
I can see them from my kitchen window.

Winter afternoons, gray days like this,
when the wind dies and the bay stills,
gray and lifeless, like granite
in a Precambrian landscape, I dream
birds back, out of season, and bird-
clatter, that hopeful beat of wings.

I conjure their small lights, those reflections
caught on a dulling bay—
and think you back, throating your song
to the one god of the mountain.

Only in these tricks of human grace,
our poem and song of particulars,
do we hold back what we can—
a dark mass of sliding hillside,
a bit of glacial till,
a feather on the beach—
in the last light thrown ashore
off a flat, undeceiving sea.

RETURNING HOME, SAXON MILLS

I walk red roads, unpaved, blowing away,
kicking leeched-dry clay. August.
Near a lake fenced with chain link,
red brick walls of the cotton mill shine
in mid-morning Southern sun.
Mama says I was born with cotton dust
in my chest. I cough once for her, once
for all my aunts and uncles.
Mama quit school at sixteen to work this mill.

"Boy, you know the hum of a spinning room,
the clack of the looms.
You know it deep in your bones."

Now in the quiet of my twenty-fourth year, I hear
the hum of the mill, and her humming
the numb walk home after shift change.
When she departs in mid-afternoon, it is 1945
and her life begins again
to stretch awake, move out into the world.
The biscuits and gravy are still there,
and the Luckies, and the soldiers on the streets
from Camp Croft, all glad the war ended.
The soldier who took her away
from the lint and heat leans on the mill gate
waiting for her. It is October, he holds
a cigarette from the wind.

This same soldier will leave her in a year.
Then she'll leave to go to Florida, to find
her family, working people, forever poor,
ready to move, carrying her clothes,
my unborn sister,
nothing left of marriage but the cheap ring.

There was her father, Lonnie, the house painter,
in Lantana. Lonnie, always drinking,
laughing at poverty. Then he was lucky.
He was always lucky. He bought good cheap land,
sold it for quick profit, a bottle,
and a fast car—headed north.
He left their world, returned years later
as a farmer in North Carolina.
In ten years he was crying, when dying of cancer,
he saw my mama, his daughter, then in her own
frame house, coming to visit a last time.
His only life bloomed in the faces of children.

There was her mama, Hulda, with breasts
hanging like sacks, who only got fatter,
sat in a wicker chair, lived like a vine
growing outward through children.
She made biscuits for breakfast,
kneaded the dough with fat hands,
washed clothes of six kids and a grandchild,
in a wringer, dried on a line under Florida sun.
The old clothes hung stiff with the heat, many sizes,
the shed skins of seven growing children.

Then mama woke in the Florida heat and it was 1952.
She caught the train north with my sister,
worked mills in the beginning of another war.
She met a man, a wanderer, who would be my father.
They married, something grew, a family and a business
pumping gas on the main highway.

In photos I've seen my father brooding—
a face stretched tight over some loss in him,
his mind working, like tonguing a hole in a tooth.
In November, the trees stiff with frost, mama
found him dead, as the running car, hose from exhaust
shook off the cold in our driveway.

Once, when I was five, my sister twelve,
in our first rented house in Spartanburg,
the three of us watched the moon circle down.
Mama sang a song to us often:

"See the Man in the Moon. Mama gonna come back soon.
But don't you worry none. She won't drink no more bad whiskey."

Now in the August heat, it's shift change.
The whistle hangs in the stiff air.
The lake stirs a moment, then is quiet.
People slip like shadows into the last
of the soft morning sun.
A man cracks his knuckles as he leaves,
another checks his head to be sure
of the billed cap
he will plow in this evening.
And I see all my uncles in the shadows—
Tommy, Norman, and the twins, Bobby and Billy,
still young and slim.
This for me is another time, but nothing changes.
The war is over, but which war?
Only now, the machines are not so loud.
Only now, the windows are bricked shut.
Then, in the last shadows, as the people thin,
I see a dark woman humming.
It could be 1945, or it could be today.
She's headed home,
humming some song she thinks I wouldn't know.

TONY DORSETT AND HIS BAND

Here you are, drunk again, and me
on a voluntary visit from Virginia,
stewing in your breath soon as I breach
the front door.
The house sways in it, this sodden dance
you choose for a week each month—
the old console stereo up so loud and hostile
that the neighbors think I've never left.

But this is not some New Wave band
or a smack of Dylan's "Homesick Blues"
riding on a needle blunt as a spool.
It's the same two smooth black albums
with dust covers somewhere filling out with dust
among paperbacks and unavoidable bills,
that tightened my throat through high school
in the middle of nights
when I would finally lose you and the world
in what resembled sleep.

Those nights Hank Williams crooned,
"Hey Good-looking" to the peeling walls,
to your face and arms bruised from falling
when you forgot your partner wasn't real.

That was pure night music, played late and warm,
the Bayou yodel and sexual tremor of old Hank
floating out on a voice rich with grease
of late-night flop houses, easy women,
and hard living.

You knew all the words and got them
right sooner or usually later than the music.
A yodel caught in your throat and broke
higher than a child's voice.

Your song floated you above all the pain
of rented houses, a husband's suicide, and years
of low-pay, workday weeks.

Now on this morning, as I return home
one more time, the other album
cracks the glass of my fatigue—
the crisp morning music,
a brass section swings in pleated-skirt,
seamed hose, dark-haired style you lost
too soon to a cotton-mill shift.
In the past year, my sister says you've taken
to calling this one Tony Dorsett and his Band.
You cheer, "Do it, Tony!" in drunken enthusiasm
like he sees a hole he could walk
his big band through—then you fill
the air with the release of your stupored body
falling through collapsible end tables,
prepared and wobbled in cases of repeat performances.

Without applause, I take you in my arms
and drag you in a slow dance we both remember
from other years and houses,
through trumpets and alto sax,
through reams of smoking air
to your bedroom to sleep off this dream week
of music one more time—
my mama, myself in the wrong light.

WRECKAGE

For Uncle Bobby

You beer-breathed oracle of quick moves
and lost friends, how did you find hours—
laying off from mill work?—to stack
boxes, beds, TV, and couch in two tight-hipped
'62 Chevy trucks to shuttle us back across town
always one last time?

I never hoped to look kindly on a childhood
of rented five-room houses, a mother
with a chronic hang-over, and roaches
not only in each greasy kitchen, but bedrooms,
halls, dens, and baths. I count back
one by one until finally the peeling wood face
of each house fills out and floats up.

In Arkwright, a fig tree with ripe
fruit, bulbed and sexual for two summers.
On Ash Street, a girl's warm breasts exposed
in the attic, taking them full-bodied
in the flushed palms of my hands.
And Uncle, they always said you two twins
grew up fast, loose, and hungry, but at only twelve
I watched the truth in the back bedroom of a neighbor's
house, warm and wet and churning.

In the years moving, I found
freedom has nothing to do with motion.
Staying in a house three years
to see my best friend out-grow his Sunday
suit, the one I might get in hand-me-downs,
beat the hell out of boredom born
in the full bed of your pick up
stacked high with the same scarred bureaus.

Every move, unsure of mama's
choice of low-rent, short-term housing,
you jerked the skids out from the rounded edges
of my fragile childhood sense of place—

"If you don't like the neighborhood, boy,
sit back, keep your motor running, and
it'll change again."

Where are you now Uncle Bobby?
It's ten years since you prayed off beer
to sign on with a wife, a bank mortgage, a trailer,
and a low-haul rig in a park of aluminum houses
on the growing end of a cotton-mill town.
Then, out of nothing, you called
last week from DC where weekly you haul
two runs from South Carolina on eighteen wheels.
Your voice seemed richer
back then, when beer-breathed stories
held me fixed to the floor.
Through a vibrating distance
of phone lines, a thousand empty rooms,
a few salvaged lives, I listened as you stammered
through your best Southern
monotone, unsure of words to use on a boy
you'd last seen seven years past
at his last family reunion before college.

Good-bye, Bobby. I know it wasn't just
a ride home you offered passing through
Virginia on your weekly haul north. But I know
whatever motivation, it was deep-seeded and warm—
my number straight from mama, stuck in your throat
as the operator returned your dime, completing the call.
It was purely that connection of kin, that twist
of the genes deeper than place or proximity,
a slow skip of sparks across distances.
You'd say a myth-sized face from my past
and a small child's shadow

was what held us there on long distance
for more than the two minutes we talked.
It was a blood-course, you're right,
and a past too large to fit,
as we stumbled through a language
the wreckage of which could not fill
any distance between us.

I should have told you things that night.
I should pressed the ragged arc
of my life into the receiver, into some raw song
you once understood. I could have said these days
I roar head-on down those same roads where you
left your beer and pick up cooling,
traded in the last duck-tail in Spartanburg
for a Sunday suit and lace shoes,
got on your knees and prayed for the fire to burn
you salt clean of all itinerant girls' thighs,
all the cold cans of beer, all the squeezed
shift knobs popped in your palm for speed.

I've looked like you did for something
so fast and perfect I could lose all sense
and bearing. I spent four years searching
solely for that sustaining speed.
I want to come full circle in world
of endless departures and returns, to call
this place something more than *tomorrow* or *years*.

Uncle, between you and me,
I'd chew nails to stop from shitting regular,
break my back to keep from standing still.
Your hope's to look around at fifty
and pray nothing changed for half your life.
Mine's to call up the past and back off from nothing.
At twenty-five I trail the ashes of fifteen houses
and a million miles of telephone poles,
call up trains and jets and buses.

You ride your long-haul rig
in the same tight circle twice a week.
I still ride around books and women
like fingers around cans of beer.
We both might arrive empty.

III. A FEW EARLY UNCOLLECTED POEMS (1980s)

SUGAR CANE

There are fields as far as a man
could run in an hour, a horse
in thirty minutes. In the time
it takes to file your blade
a truck from the horizon pulls up
at your feet, a rise of red dust
settling slowly behind.

You watch. You, the one with no shirt.
The one who shits where he works,
whose machete like a part of your arm
hacks the cane three times. It falls,
stripped of leaves and halved.
You move on. Again, the same motion.
And again the same. Then the gathering and loading.
This all day until the sun drops.
You've been at it since dawn.
For your work there is six dollars Belize.

In the distance, the Tower Hill Refinery
smokes and fumes over fields of ripe cane.
In the trucks, the drivers wait their turn
to unload. They eat mangos, drink warm beer.
A small boy sells ice from a can.
On the shelves in Orange Walk Town,
the sugar is no cheaper than flour
from wheat grown and milled in the north.

But you work the fields as far as you can see
in the heat, then walk home in the cool
and at night dream drifts of green cane,
your blade, like a part of you always
leading into the only life you know.

SAN ANTONIO, CAYO DISTRICT

This close to the border, he says
he would shoulder a shotgun against
Guatemalans and holds two thick fingers
against his flat palm to show at least
this many would die before he finally fell
for his children, the dark ones.

"I am Mayan," and his thumb presses
his chest. He draws a local beer
into his mouth as the truck he owns
and runs between villages rocks forward.

He asks, "What of you Americans selling arms
to the Guats?" and our lives circle
like unknown birds in his eyes.
We look at our hands.

He tells of the British, "We are a Crown Colony,"
their Harrier fighter planes, and shows
a take off, the way his people mime
animals with their hands. "VTOL!"
He bellows. "Only two things make
Thunder—God and the white man!"

This close to the border it is all field talk:
slash and burn for ash, a bag of seed
for next year's corn, shadow columns crossing
the Macal river at night.

He leans close. "I tell you this:
it will happen late some May before the rains come."

JUNGLE TRAINING SCHOOL, MACAL RIVER

For Ab Abercrombie

Out here, brush grows up so fast
they carry machetes to breakfast
to find the cook stove.
We squat by a low stick fire, drink tea,
eat crackers and cheese soft in the heat.
All of the men speak at once.
They want to know why we walk in this far.
We are the first white ones in a week.

We say we are naturalists. In Augustine
someone said there were crocs on the river.
We came for that and hopes of seeing macaws
in the early mornings.

They say they have seen both, show us
a skin from a croc drying in the sun,
and two macaws tied to a perch. The two
birds are a tangle of red and green.

Then they tell us of thirty men in the mountains,
young recruits from England.
"They sleep in their pants, cut fresh trails
for a week. We find them twice a day.
An ambush is set. They learn to be quick
with live rounds singing near. Keeps 'em low!"

In a few minutes we stand to leave.
They coax us to return for tea in the morning.

Near the river we find a flat place
where a British tank made a trail
and camp there. At dusk we hear snap
and roll of gunfire in the mountains,
like thunder coming on. "M-16s,
Ab says, "listen to that song."

And I know then, the only peace
in this country is parrots settling
in trees, a clear light at dawn,
and this talk between men,
knowing tea is on the stove.

REPTILES TEACH HIM ABOUT HUNTING:
NOTES ON CATCHING CROCODILES IN BELIZE

After years dragging through streams
in South Carolina, I find my friend here:
David, prone across the bow of a canoe,
his headlamp the only light, breath falling,
rising with each paddle beat from the stern,
hands motionless over the dark marsh water.

He fixes the croc's red eyes in his lamp,
whispers, "It's still up." The pineal body
takes over, crawling out through the marsh,
to play an old game. Ahead, the croc floats
secure in the one sure eye of the lamp.

Is it up?
It's still up.

Or it's late on a dry-season night
like this me, with no moon and you
are the croc hunting for pond turtles.
Then another hunter hauls his canoe
from a hiding spot a half-mile inland
and slaps you with light. You spark red, stay up,
until the light in you blinks out as buck shot
cracks the tight bone of your skull.

He strips your belly skin, sells it
to the local hide dealer for enough Belizian
dollars to feed his family a week.
The canoe stops. David moves quickly,
grabs snout. It twists loose, larger
than he thought, pulls him in, then is gone.
"Shit," David snorts. "Shit. I had a big one."

He stands, old fatigues dripping, rising
from another age, the light focused
on a finger where a croc tooth pulled blood.
Then he throws the arm of light over the marsh,
looking for shines, the old game,
how all this goes on.

ALONG THE LITTLE BETSIE

for Nikki and Dan

If in your indifference you have mistaken
these lines for a river in northern Michigan, return
to the beginning of the poem. Or if you find brown trout here,
eddies, or caddisfly larvae drifting along
the margins, cast them out like abstraction.

There will be no river in this poem. No remnant wilderness
encountered, or left behind. Return to the beginning
if you admit disappointment at the poverty of
narrative or image, rhyme or meter, the poet's common speech
in which we fool or startle the world's approach.

If you have followed this far and see two ducks
hiding in shallows, admit they are only ducks
in the imagination, not named, given genus or species.

Snow falling. Early afternoon. I am walking in the woods
along the Little Betsie. Hear the snow like a broom
sweeping a hardwood floor? Are you so easily fooled?
Return to the beginning. How can it be
a broom sweeping the woods that slope to a river
not in this poem? I hope you are not there
on the banks of the Little Betsie, for you are here,
if my speech has trailed you this far.

For those among you who have yet to see a river
you do not need my permission to proceed.
But if a river flows here for you, return once more
to the beginning and do not repeat your mistake.

You can make no mistake; if you see a river
between here and there, you will return again.

If you are somehow here, so full of joy to have lost
the Little Betsie, you have learned a new skill, to clear
things up, the difference between what is
and what is not, like the river, far from you
which in your indifference you have allowed to be.

READING REYNOLDS PRICE

If the world exists it is
just outside Lovingston, Virginia.
It is not like my memory,
this walking backwards in strong winds.

First the fox was in front
of the car, then in the fields across
the county road, circling left
with a flock of quail.

Plunge in, I urged from my speeding
machine. Bless the rough ground.
Risk the warmth.

CHEKHOV VISITS MY KITCHEN

I settle into chopping, rock the knife
through celery, the snap of green pepper.
In the open window, pods of garlic push
past sprouting pearl onions, and leeks
soak in tap water, cut thin to stew
with mussels cleaned in the stainless sink.

In the nineteenth century, you talked of love
by saying, "Next day they had delicious pies,
crayfish, and mutton chops, and during the meal,
Nikanor, the cook, came upstairs to inquire
what the guests would like for dinner."

Fresh thyme. Garlic drips through red juice
as moist meat turns over an open fire.
Nearby, Nikanor cuts small carrots
like orange nickels to fill the pies.

We both cook to set things right inside,
the way vegetables taste in season.
When friends come I offer wine
and the day's luster in conversation—
fresh crayfish are never in the market here.
Asparagus is two dollars a pound
and hard to find as love.

SHOPPING

For Mike Delp

Every purchase a little wildness
goes out of us
and the world gets smaller.

Shampoo, Q-tips, rice cakes.
Pushing the cart
we've already dammed
a river inside us,
strip-mined ten acres.

Suppose we pulled back,
found a dry cave, ate huckleberries,
cooked pan fish on a flat rock?

The world still surrounds us.
Only in some distant kingdom
would people pass the racks of *Time*.

But just beyond
the electric doors and cinder walls
a blue sky is hidden by clouds.
The smaller we get
the more we buy.

SITTING IN THE KITCHEN

I love the smell of morels drying
in the window. They keep me sitting longer.
The old woman cut loose from care, wandering
Spring Street every morning in rolled nylons
and an open, black coat, is no cause to abandon
this early light where my coffee steams.

All things need practice. Why scrub the scum
from between the kitchen tiles unless you plan
to wear their grid through the days, loving the memory
of mildewed grout, a map for a country of work and silence?

This morning, I'm loving smaller things, and they
are in love with me. Keith Jarrett scores
the woman's stagger as the cats pace the back porch,
wanting in. Animal need and the needle's delicate
tracking make a music which surprises. Even a skip
on side two is something to count on through the breeze.

My friends tell me I sometimes get words wrong.
Sierra is not a desert, and more is the opposite
of less, not at all like an eel. But I'm paying
attention now. Last night I asked my friend Coleman
how he felt. He said, "Empty but good." This is different
and small, but worth remembering.

IV. from *AS THE WORLD AROUND
US SLEEPS* (1991)

CHOPPING WOOD

I split what remains of the woodpile,
seeking the sanity of the familiar,
the rough music of repetition;
pounding the stuck axe deeper in oak,
each wetwood sound issues
assurance for the need of this work.

But collecting unsplit: the thick-
knotted pine slabs, forked hickory,
the twist-grained oak chunks,
their tops beaten flat and fibrous
by maul and axe, thrown to the side
of the deep-cleaved chopping stump
for winter to split and weaken.
Knots of grievance, they hiss
a sour sap as they thaw.

FOUR OLD GRAVES IN THE VIRGINIA WOODS

The planted pine forest loses its last green
to the hands of the woman beside me.
She takes small stalks of heal-all and aster
to sketch in the evening, of this, the first
day of a fast-fading October.

Only then, slowly searching the underbrush,
do we sense the ordered row of quartz markers
and sunken ground beside them.
We touch the first stone to find some chiseled
omen of that gone life and find only
cool, fractured crystalline rock.

We open our hands and measure the concave vault
of ground where the coffin sank into itself,
where breast and bone gave way in the heat
of that first summer under grass.
Now, only saplings rise out of the long-settled
graves; I pull one out at the roots,
shake it, smell thick, black humus.

Then, we both stretch out
 in the hollow bowls opened there.
Above, as when we were children
on our backs in cool backyards,
clouds flush and roll in the green limbs
of pines, until we close our eyes,
and the earth below, as it always did,
rises in the reverse rhythm of clouds.

Then our eyes warm open
with the dull cast of late sun in our faces.
As if a last child's game has ended,
we look at each other and laugh—
lying out, as we are, among graves.

THE COUNTRY HOUSE

Even here, deep in our overgrown
country yard fenced by cedars
I can't lose the suburban drone
of a mower making an agreeable
lawn, establishing order.
The mower cuts back fresh grass
of spring, uncovers my first
junctured childhood memories:
the April after my father's suicide,
me five, and the grass gone to seed
around our frame house in North
Carolina; my mother practicing her
loneliness in a whiskey bottle.
By fall, we had left that house,
leaving the brown, broomstraw lawn
unbroken, but beaten flat with use,
over lost boards, long-necked
bottles, abandoned toys.

★

Last week wind lifted yellow
pollen from the branches of cedars
and you laughed, never knowing
before that moment of spring's
first sexual movements, tactile
as the dust covering the car,
the cats, the ground between us.
Then in your face was the flush
of grave awareness: so much lost
in that clumsy mating of conifers.
You shook your hair and walked
inside, giving up the day.

★

At four a.m. my mother called
and I stood in the blowing darkness
hearing the same denials
of my life away from her.
She is still practicing loneliness
and the phone keeps some hold
on the child I was, keeps her close
to the one *who would never leave,*
never twist her grief back to its source—
that emptiness again—
never mirror her pain with anger,
only take it in, hold it deep inside.
Even the frogs near the pond
knew sadness when it came like
human voices through the night;
they rattled *grief, grief,*
as I talked Mama down from a white
hell of her own isolation.
I gripped the wood rail of the porch
and tried to ground the pain I felt
in something solid, something
once rooted and green.

                              ★

Late last night with you away
working third shift at the hospital,
I read William Bartram's *Travels,*
lost in a world of first light
where North America stretched
wild and balanced into the purity
of animal and vegetable indifference.
Tennessee was the prop for every sunset,
and Asheville, just another border town.
I stepped out on the front porch
half expecting deer or even bison
in the cleared space of our yard,
but across the acres of darkened
second-growth forest and gravel roads

I caught the rank lowing of cattle,
the car lights scything the highest cedars.

        ★

The noisy neighbor mows
up and down his lawn as ragged
evening shadows stain the small pond.
I fish, for only in fishing, and the soothing
repetition of cast and spin cast and spin
can I forget it is April and in a month
I will be gone.

I cannot see you lost inside the house,
moving in the occupied rhythm of your own
indifference ever since the light
between us failed.

I stand, reeling
in a small bass to throw back
and the sun disappears.
For a second, the air goes
perceivably still. The mower stops
worrying the evening
with its own pitch of sanity.

THE DISTANCES

While I was gone south, the dull spade
of waking, each morning, unearthed
the wrong stones: a black burst
drifted among the quilts and sunlight
until you saw birds, dreamed angels.
Two figures, twin and electric,
walked toward the back fence with us
watching, sure of something,
some part of us made otherwise,
lost in the dream's distance.

When I returned, you repeated the two
recurrent dreams and details gathered
something green darkened by shadow,
and us aware of an immense free thing
finally revealed. And in both dreams
"the distances" and within distances,
tricks of perspective: the earth seen
from a vulture's eyes, the huge black bird
tightening circles in the revolving world
above our field, and you, caught somewhere
between the earth and a retreating light
that walked as we do.

SIX LANDSCAPES FROM A CIVIL WAR

Driving north to Manassas
the young man saw brown fields
and stone walls of Virginia's
Rt. 29 as a collodion print
by Matthew Brady. The young woman

beside him asked, "What is that bird
with the red spot?" Ignoring her question
he answered, "I was always disappointed

at the slowness of the film: Union
soldiers swollen and twisted, caught
among a blur of blown shrubs,
the wrecked farms. The old camera
always just missed focus on
a farmer's sad family." She answered,
"Clouds the color of iron, land
the color of clouds, and us, the color of land."

                         ★

Once, months before, near the end
of September, they sat on the porch
of their small house in the country
and read pages of Whitman's
Civil War poems to the frogs,
to the drooping cedars, to each other.
She acted out a soulful "Cavalry
Crossing a Ford," and beat the stresses
on the railing when he read a booming
"Blow! Bugles! Blow!" Afterwards,
they made love, their worlds
meshed in a simpler music.

                         ★

Before their trips to battle fields,
he always tested her on the Civil War:

Q. First important battle?
The Wilderness.

Q. How many sides were there?
Three. Ironclad and Blockade were two.

Q. The Gettysburg Address?
*Miss Scarlet, I don't know nothing
'bout birthin no baby!*

Q. What about Manassas?
*Steven Stills' third album.
The train stopping on our trip
to Washington. Breakfast being served.*

★

As they walked the trail down
Bull Run he thought how shallow
it looked. She watched
the dog eddy out behind a log,
then swim into the current again.
A child walked past them, stopped,
asked if the dog was theirs. *Mine,*
she said. Then the child wanted
to know about the bulls. Did they
know where to see the bulls?
"Jesus," she laughed, "he wants
to know about the bulls!"

★

Chinn Ridge, Matthews Hill, Stone Bridge,
Sudley Springs, Farm Ford all danced
off a red map as they walked
the points of interest marked by bronze

stars. From the ridge near the visitor
center, they saw the plugged barrels
of cannon aimed at Henry House,
and the tourists nearby fascinated
with the raw workings of battle.

The young man pushed a button
and cannon fire rattled from the base
of Jackson's statue, and a voice
said, "*Rally behind the Virginians!*"
The young man read from the guide book—
"Not once, but twice, the battles
bloodied Chinn Ridge, 1861, and '62—"
and he tingled with the life of it.
The young woman asked, "The dog.
Have you seen Nellie?"

★

Before they left, a blue Yankee
sky slipped south softening gray
hues of winter. They watched the dog
chase a stick thrown across the kept
grass of Manassas; but "Go get it!"
was lost among the wafting scents
from the battles buried under their feet.
The dog ran, nose to ground, past

the stick, past Jackson's statue
where he stood in bronze like a stone
wall with his back bent under
the full weight of his name.
If he could laugh from his small,
push-button voice box
he would, sensing the oddness of the scene:

the young man filling the blank horizon
with conflicts, the woman laughing,
and the dog keeping close to dry grass,
all lost in their separated pleasures.

THE SMALL LOSSES

I wanted to speak for all
the small losses between us,
to warm the space around
our separated silences
with some simple luminous clarity.
Once I said the word *skunk* and saw
your face warm to a place, a particular
night when you lost all bearing
and swerved past the black and white
elegance caught in your killing lights.
Or the time you did not miss
and the stiff spice of skunk
sat in the car for nearly a week
like some other body between us.

I am reminded of a field we saw
where a thousand scattered flecks
of black took to the air.
Birds, you said, *thousands.*
My mind rushed through every name.
Starlings, I said, *grackles,*
finches, wrens, crows.
I tried them all, each
with a hope of some surety.
Then something in that selfish
dance of naming left a cold field
separating us. The birds
had left before we caught
much more than a spray
of black to carry home.
That night you said *thousands*
and my mind searched a winter
field for something lost.

But this morning I listen
to you in the kitchen rolling
out dough, pounding the greasy lump
between palms brown with flour.

You are making our bread,
you are measuring our lives,
pressing them into loaves.

The rhythmic pounding is a song
you want to keep from me:

This is the flour of mornings together.
This, the milk of longing.
This, the perfect egg you said we'd make
between us in darkness.
And my hands like sledges of winter ice
break down the meaning
of separate longings and work
it to make all one.

Out my window I watch a small
finch pinch berries off cedars.
I trace its red flick in and out
of shadows in branches.
This morning it should be quieted
from its animal freedom,
it should be caged,
there should be hunts and stews.

MEMORY

A cold morning,
rhododendron leaves
drooped close to stems,
mud banks turned crystal
in a stiff, January wind.
I remember a barn
where I made love
in a high loft one summer

dawn as black swallows
slipped through the shadows,
two tight bodies turning.

The cool morning rose
through slatted wood walls
and she left to wash
and dress. I watched
her back leaving the bed.
That clear dawn never again.

KEELMEN HEAVING COALS BY MOONLIGHT

We swayed within a field of light,
selfish by our definitions,
carrying its limits like a twin
body around us. Walking the galleries
our fingers were latticed in the pocket
of my faded army jacket. When opened,
our hands' seam was the line
across caring and indifference; closed,
they hinged a fold of light between us.

Looking at Turner's painting, unsure
of what our eyes were given, you guessed
"the moon is the light's source."

But the moonlight seemed radiant beyond
any night I could remember. It was more
like a persistent morning light that once,
before you woke, visited your face until
your arm's shadow absorbed its company.

"If not the moon, then the keelmen's fires."

But those workers stood harnessed to furnaces,
ignoring an expanse of stoked light bending
behind their shirtless bodies. Like us,

they fed a hot, sustaining flame. How innocent
it seemed and so futile: to tend such small
fires, burning against that quantum sky
and the presence of such light.

CHICORY BROUGHT INSIDE

Chicory, I beseech you. Settle in. Sit and drink. Sip. Sip.
Don't be a blue deceiver. I have seen you a bolt of sky
shot to earth, but your color comes and goes, like a guest
unsure of the sincerity of her welcome.

There are friends in the bathroom: Fleabane on the tank;
each flush applauds the sureness of its white!
And the dining room table flaunts a stand of Queen Anne's
finest lace. Even the flies attend it.

But chicory, you offer me a faded white
the color of cheap soap.

Will you come back with the sun, or do I have to pick
more, try again? Oh how you strut in the wind
on roadsides as I drive by; hold back your blue shout,
your taunting azure stare wide as the sky!

Unruly flower: now in the morning air and birdsong,
you return with your blue gift like a giddy lover.

BROWN'S COVE: THE EIGHTIES BEGIN

Listen to the pipes thaw,
to the last pine logs spit
in the stoves: the music of poverty,
I think, the rhythms of the poor.

But the romance disappears
as snow-melt shows the hillsides,
leaving an offering of crushed cans
and foam rubber the color of flesh.

Our car takes a curve
and slows behind a pick up stopped
in the road. The driver gets out
and loads a dead deer, meat for winter.

I accelerate between two hills
slouched like watchmen, like closing gates.

ROAD GANG

The man with the shotgun
propped on his belly
has work to get done, watches each man
swing the bush ax, hack with the slingblade,
sumac and mullein falling before them.

Cars whisper past a young prisoner
with kinky blond hair. Reflections
are the faces he hates, from childhood
slowly drifting past into the present.

He looks up:
at noon the only shadow
is the hawk hunting above.

BUILDING THE PHEASANT CAGE

"No more damn everything depending on me,"
each word punctuates the air with a hammer blow.
I am about to marry his daughter, and he,
about to leave her mother, as we stand in collapsing
light, building a cage for pheasants.

The women move in the kitchen, cooking supper.
"It's nearly ready, Honey," his wife calls.
He turns the hammer in his hand, takes a drink
of warm beer. "Maybe I can live in this cage.
Have for years anyway."

His hospital beeper hangs in his shirt pocket, waiting
to call him away to the women he helps.

We've been working for hours with little progress
and light has a skill for putting an end
to things going on too long. "Let's call it,"
he says but then turns.

He hammers one more nail. "You know,
birds ain't a damn thing like women." I agree,
though not knowing what he means.

"Don't let anyone ever tell you that crap."

MORNING

Last night we ran two miles down our gravel road
past the house and yard, through newly tasseled corn,
past a paddock where two thoroughbreds looked
like Pleistocene camels, laying their ears back
in the cool, night wind, through a hollow so dark,
we stepped lightly, hoped the road didn't fall away
as the sun fell; the dogs saw another landscape

and ran head-on, unafraid of the darkness, smelling
for skunks or rabbits out to feed. We topped the hill.
An electric throb of lights at the Del Monte plant
shocked us and the fields with a sulfurous glow
I cannot connect with the living.

I remember a night walk through oaks on the marsh side
of Cumberland Island where I was stopped in a similar glow
from flood lights across grass and salt water
at the King's Bay Trident Submarine Base. I forgot
the owls I followed through the forest and stood
instead in silence left by tree frogs and insects
fooled by false morning;

each time, before even the dogs or owls had noticed
the change, I wished for darkness again,
a pure summer night of seconds earlier, before
the invention of light.

CYCLE

Let live oaks grow up
and I'll become those trees
When the best of being is spread
among the sphagnum moss and leaves,
let no one see that place and call
it place, but simply let it be.

PINELANDS

I am not the mouse stunned
in the field, am not the piglet
stopped by the snake's strike
headed north on the still trail.

I listen for the singing tail.
When the snake sings I stop,
the way a hawk gliding above
attends the long, summer grass.

My shadow makes palmetto sing:
call me darkness falling over song.

ON PRATT'S TRAIL

I want to know the sleep
of beasts in a field,
to lie in a ragged grove
and feed the live oak's hunger
If the insects want me,
let them come. I give up
my life, a skin being shed,
then grow it back,
and give it over again.

STAFFORD BEACH

Orb Weaver suspended within
an intricate web.
Her strands form a circle
in the right slanting light.
Then, from both sides,
another slant of lines
connect like paths on a map.

Along one strand
a male spider heads back
toward her, stops in a grid
of light, then turns,
remembering the way.

EATING OYSTERS

Aboriginals with screwdrivers,
we plunder clusters
until the thick, slurried hinges give.

Inside, the dry seals glitter,
pearl bowls hoard a blue translucence,
and flesh-bulbs, jowl-thick,
ride tides of brown marsh draught.

We drink salt libations, brine baths
slopped from the deepest shells,
slice each crimped dollop free.

You slurp out flat half-moons;
I tear loose the wet lips with my teeth.

EARLY SPRING ON CUMBERLAND ISLAND

For David Scott

Friends for ten years, we know without saying
to walk the edges, to watch ahead for herons,
to check the low limbs of willows for snakes.
You motion across the marsh's width and I wade,
waist-deep in stained water, to where you've
stopped a cottonmouth at the margin of grass
and dry deer path, and with your simple presence
twisted the snake into its quick defensive coil.
Then it strikes deep and decisively, but misses,
directed toward the nearest pocket of heat.
I want to joke with our first words in an hour
that now we can be sure another spring is here,
that our first snake each year calls back
long days and warm nights, the click of cricket
frogs, and the quickening crawl of green.

SEEING WILD HORSES

If only I could tell you how wildness shows
the space between us and the green world;
how an island is the same island with our
presence, but with that presence we lose
some hope of seeing, say, a horse, or the dead
gnarled limbs of an oak sunk in sand.

Edward Weston saw it in the folds of a pepper
and tried to hold not the succulent essence
of vegetable richness, but to take the divorce,
the gap between pepper and tripoded camera,
and catch purely the third thing,
the twisted surface perfect and singular.
Like now, soon after I wake I see

on the beach, unexpected, between sea
and shifting dunes, among the drifts
of kicking sand, horses running past, intent
on some distant grazable stand of island grass,
the word stall only a hiss in my mouth.
And to realize I've seen a wild horse the first

time, a swift knot of freedom, and I fight
some need to call it from that animal world,
then lose it in the shock of its leaving;
I call this the greed of human caring,
and count all my losses among its history.

V. *BODY POEMS* (1988)

THE BODY IS DEEPER THAN WE THINK

I'm thinking of my body as a deep cave.
Just under the skin is light like dawn,
heading toward evening the deeper I go.
Somewhere in here even the light stops.
A friend once walked me into his dark room
and we passed through two giant locks,
tight right angles of cement and tile.
"Light does not turn corners."
He smiled, deep in that private darkness.

Inside my body, sounds that I left behind
like the clock ticking or a car stopped on the street
are far away as light in other galaxies.

Already I'm so far inside, thinking this way,
that water does not know where to run
to the surface. Down here thought and time
and the space between my feet are all
the same: if I get back it could be tomorrow
or yesterday or the moment between.

THE BODY IS FULL OF LINES

1.

Waiting in line for some word from the world.
It's been years since the good boys went off to the war.
Yet I still wait for them to call my number.
I'd go to the front if someone would point the way.
Necessity is still the better part, but the line
gets longer the longer I need.

2.

The woman all wear red hats with feathers
and wait in longer lines for the things they want.
Here at least there is some ghost of order.
Men whose needs are deeper than mine
push carts from end to end
selling fish of the day. Who will stop
a ceremony of such sad innocence, where a man
can drown in his own commerce?

3.

A man whose need is no greater than mine
tells me there is still no news from the front.
It is not the distance I want to cross
though the women watch from a distance.

4.

At the front, men talk quietly around fires.
Here women talk quietly among themselves.
They burn like fires as they stand in line.
Across the distance I smell their smoke.
The feathers sway on their hats like a line of flame.

5.

It is cold here. We stomp our feet to stay warm
and hide our hands under great coats.
The women talk.
From this distance it sounds like birds in a field.
The small doves of their speech hover between us.

THE BODY IS FULL OF ANIMALS I'VE NEVER SEEN

Some nights I can feel them passing inside.
They keep close to the walls of my sleep.
Their presences make shadows on waking,
but I'm not fooled.

These are animals so full of the inner world
they pad through the dark and leave
no tracks in the body's clearings.
My yawns leave their breath in the room.

THE BODY IS FULL OF SORROW

Thirsty for the drops of water on the ceiling
I have given up the space between.
Sitting in a chair with a cotton cover
I wish it wool instead.
In the deep groove of winter,
snow is like sun in a hot time.
I have given up memory's thick air
for ice shacks on the lake.
All this and I have begun an impossible
love affair with apples. There is space
in me for a full moon. None of this is metaphor.
It is all image and narrative. I have willed
it to a priest with a cabin in Maine.
And this foot? It will not fail me as you have.
It will walk long hours over ice for a friend.

THE BODY IS FULL OF WATER

In the vapor rising from our bodies
is carried the great salt sea of our flesh-time.
On the lake where the moons of rain gather
and disappear I see the flames of falling
water and the ice of waves.

This is not the story of each moment,
not the pulse, or the tide receding.
This is the rhythm that was:
the oxbow in the river, the marsh miles inland,
the force that cut the cliffs, not the sea below.

THE BODY IS FULL OF GOOD FISHING

This is an old dream my body has hidden for years:
for every mammal in me, there is also a fish.
Unlike me, they all breathe both air and water equally.
This does not matter. In the dark body, there is both.
When I go visit I feel my way between the two places
with my hands, which have always known the difference.

There is no need for flies. Or a fly rod made
of the finest bamboo. I make my way among the fish,
walking the sea my body leaves behind when it wakes.
There is no light, but I know each fish wears
my face, and like me, has hands to help
as they move between my body's dark chambers.

I have seen fish outside the body, and assume
I can walk among schools as on a reef.
When I approach, they bend around me like light.
When they pass, deep in the body I feel the water's wind.

THE BODY IS FULL OF LOVERS

Some way she can lay herself open like a field
is the last thing he wants.
For her the moon rising means weeks of warmth.
Twice they went to the grocery store
with the moon out and she walked the aisles crying.

Time for him is old socks in a drawer,
shirts that never are white again.
For her it opens like the leaves on a magnolia,
green even in winter.

What would happen if he turned
at the right moment and they heard the same sound?
Like water through stones
or the knowledge that something had moved?

What he wants is ground packed on ground
with nothing but the sky above.
"Be a mining engineer," she says.

Some day he *will* mine the moon, he says.
Bring it back for her, name it,
"Dead stone moving through a dark sky."
Then stand, tossing her moon from hand to hand.

THE BODY IS FULL OF PARABLES

Turn the skins of women electric
and the earth wobbles. Turn the skins
of men to iron and the earth looks the same.
Even a man cries when not touched
but still he plants in the spring.
In the valley the wind blows.
The swans on the bay
do not move from the coves.

The heart is a plough no woman
can claim only for her fields.

THE BODY IS FULL OF THE VOICES OF CHILDREN

I hear them in the woods of my sleep.
They cry with voices like broken glass.
Each time I turn to see them, they are
mist at noon. Their words are separate
and distinct as leaves on a tree,
but the tree cannot be named.

I call to them in a language of the living
but each time the sound drifts through
their hair like wind. "Listen," I want to say.
"Pull closer so you can hear."

VI. from *AGAINST INFORMATION*
   & OTHER POEMS (1995)

SOMEDAY MY MOTHER'S DEATH

will be the mistletoe in the oak, will be the way mistletoe
sends out runners in the living wood, the way it stays green
when everything around it turns brown, will be her stories popping
white berries in our memories, especially Christmas, how even
after the mistletoe kills the oak it goes on living high
in the tree for years.
                                    And the old woman when she dies
will remember the persistence of mistletoe, the rough leaves
sprigs of mistletoe good for nothing beyond the everyday
pleasure of looking out the upstairs window into the highest
branches, choked with mistletoe, sad with mistletoe, last
great breath of oak before the mistletoe goes the way of oak.

CONNEMARA

After a Steichen photograph of the Sandburgs

Maybe they sit outside, after feeding the goats.
She still adores him, the poet, the man with guitar
player's fingers and white hair of the far north.
His blue eyes focus off somewhere to the left,
and he holds the guitar as if a minor chord
he used to know, the difficult one, has escaped.

He has been playing folk songs. The words escaped
somehow from the mountains around them, like goats
loose in the hickory woods. And the last chord
to linger in the air drifts back toward the guitar
and settles like dust from a mote just to the left
of where her hand would rest were it extended north.

They lived for fifty years near Chicago, way north
of Connemara, but then they packed papers, escaped
the cold and the memory of the old work with the Left.
Now less interested in politics, more in baby goats,
he strums at old labor tunes on a battered guitar.
If only he could remember the tone of that lost chord.

When a boy, he only learned one simple chord
a day and stopped after a week. In the north,
where he grew up, in a railroad town, an old guitar
was less useful than a signal lantern. If you escaped
you did it by train. That slight shadow, is it goats?
Something dark does wander in the photo to the left.

By the photo's moment, he's finished Lincoln, the Left
abandoned, home and poetry, his song book's true chord.
She works in the barn. The first prizes won by goats
garland the rafters in her office. Up there, north,
it is only the cold she thinks they escaped
when they drove the truck south with stock and guitar.

For the photograph, he picks up the old guitar
and she takes her place just to the photo's left.
The goats, except for a shadow, have almost escaped
and silence is the shudder caught between the chord
lost and the chord abandoned. It's cold in the north
and she always claimed the south is better for goats.

A man once played guitar. His life was one chord.
What's lost in the photo. Later he forgot the north,
escaped the frame, the fence, like a mountain goat.

DEATH

Warm for a week, the new moon two weeks away,
          another spring storm moving in from the west,
sparrows choosing aimlessly among debris in the yard,
          as if winter had suddenly vanished. I imagine
he—the man I'm always writing about—is watching
          sparrows on a similar evening, far from home,
the sales job where he is often promoted. But it's
          the parking lot of a Wendy's on the outskirts
of Charlotte. He is my age, but older really, the way
          men age who take life seriously, stock portfolios,
suits, and cars with high resale value, a wife, children.

He has ordered off the Value Menu, a Single, large fries,
          an iced tea. Outside, sparrows dismantle a corner of bun
among the gravel and he thinks of a young woman
          in his regional office, just out of college, and how
when he sees her, each week, he remembers making love
          to his wife the first time, the desire sunk so deep
even a sparrow could not peck it out. He flirts
          a little, and once, in an elevator they were pushed
so close that he thought desire would explode from within,
          her grey suit and pantyhose blown away with one glance.

Spring is a tiny death, I say, with much joy. The slumber
          of winter falling away as chills drain back into
the earth from which they came. There are sprouts
          in the yard conjuring summer, slumbering worms.
This man within me, he has three more stops to make
          before circling home for the evening. He thinks
of the young woman in the office a final time, a last
          French fry from his Value Meal. Does she eat
alone? With friends from the office? His wife waits,
          the furnace set at 65, dinner on the stove.

I get up to make coffee a final time this morning,
            another set of grounds for the compost. I would
never choose to be anywhere but here.

SWEET TEA

God rested on the seventh day, but early in the morning,
      before the sun strained into the Southern sky,
      she made sweet tea from scratch. She boiled the water
      in a black kettle, put in the orange pekoe bags
      and let them stand as the water perked, and then
      she did what gods know to do: she heaped in Dixie
      Crystal sugar while the brew was still warm as the day.

For God so loved the world she made sweet tea. For she served
      the tea to anyone who admired her creation. To anyone
      walking down the street of the wet new neighborhood,
      to the mailman delivering early on that next day
      of that second week, to the milkman in his truck, the black
      man working in the yard, to the white man selling peaches
      door to door. On God's sidewalk there was an X scratched
      by hobos. They knew to come to God's back door and you'd
      get a plate of leftovers and all the sweet tea you could
      drink. They knew the sugared pints of contentment. They drank
      sweet tea from God's back steps and went on their wandering
      way again.

For God knows sweet tea fills with love and refreshment from
      any long train. For sweet tea is safe as an oak forest
      camp. Sweet tea, clinks in jelly jars. Sweet tea,
      sweeter as it stands. For God's sake we brew it
      like religion. For God's sake we carry it now in Styrofoam
      cups in cars. We drink it in winter. We drink it always.

And this poem would not lessen sweet tea's place in the creation.
      Sweet tea is not fading from the Southern towns
      like the Confederate flag. It lives in houses all over town.
      Black folk brew it often as white folk. Take the flag off
      the state capitol. It doesn't mean anything to me.
      But leave me my sweet tea, a recipe for being civil.

This poem stands cold sweet tea up as God's chosen beverage.
    The manifest Southern brew. When sad I draw figures
    in the condensation of glasses of sweet tea. I connect
    the grape leaves on the jelly jar, cast out any restaurant
    that will not make it from scratch. When lonely I go
    to the house of my beloved.

For I love a woman who makes sweet tea late at night to eat with
    Chinese food. For her hands move like God's through the ritual.

For it is as if she had learned it along with speaking in
    tongues. For I love the way her hands unwrap the tea bags
    and drop them in the water. For I love the unmeasured sugar
    straight from the bag, the tap water from deep in the earth.
    For the processes are as basic as making love.

For our bodies both are brown like suntans inside from years
    of tea. For sweet tea is the Southern land we share, the town,
    the past. When we kiss, it is sweet tea that we taste as
    our lips brush. When we are hot, it is sweet tea we crave.
    When we have children, it will be sweet tea.
    And they will learn tea along with Bible stories and baseball.

AGAINST INFORMATION

I. NEW SATELLITE DISHES

Today the next satellite dish is announced,
"pizza-sized," 18 inches across, pulls in
150 channels, mounts on the rooftop, railing,
windowsill, $699.95, includes decoder box
and remote control.

This is the latest machinery. This is the council of technicians.
    User friendly. Installs in minutes. No adjustments necessary.
    Lifetime guarantee. Call now for a free demonstration.
    1-800-555-DISH. The greatest innovation since the tractor.
    Get rid of the old dish in your yard. Plant seedlings
    in it. You out there in Iowa, feed your hogs from the bowl.
    In California, fill it with water for a pool, or put it
    in the barn, in the attic like your grandmother's hatbox.

The old dish is the Olduvai Gorge of past entertainment,
    the last empire charged on your credit card, the Hindenburg
    of information, the Pony Express of movies, the siege
    catapult of sports. This is the Age of Information
    and smaller machinery clears all misunderstandings about
    who won the Series, the latest theories on evolution,
    the number of American medals at the Olympics, the sexual
    orientation of Michael Jackson, and who is president.
    Right now someone is mounting the new pizza dish,
    somewhere else there is an English muffin dish, a silver
    dollar dish, a dish the size of a dime. And next
    to the easy chair rests a new decoder with 500 channels.

And from the glowing screen somewhere a man speaks in a hundred
    voices about the coming of Christ, another of the Serengeti,
    another of measles and the Home Pharmacy. Don't open
    your hearts to *Car Talk*. Fall on your knees for diversity.
    Don't punch from AM to FM. The pale hand taps a remote,
    the circuits respond like Lippinzaner stallions. In Sarajevo
    the radio broadcasts men walking through snow. The signal

bounces off cloud cover, huddles like rats in the condensers.

On cable a former beauty queen adjusts her makeup, air time
    moments away, the satellites poised above, the recoilless
    rifles asleep in caves in the hillside. The howitzers
    trundling over dust to the rear. The beauty queen's
    waist is thin as a mortar shell. Her technician counts
    to ten backwards as the satellite pivots in space.

Welcome to the war. Welcome to the future. Welcome
    all of you out there in Iowa who have just tuned in.
    I lift a signal from one of the former garden spots.
    I stand here lighter than the year I won the title.
    I laugh when it is appropriate. I bleed when called.
    My blond hair is styled in the midst of war and rape.
    My fingernails are not broken. I'd eat three squares
    if not dieting. I'd fly to Paris to diddle my boyfriend.
    I'd drink water hauled by some jet from some other world.

II. RÉSUMÉS FOR POETS

Yesterday in the mail a friend sends ten résumés
of poets, dense, endless lists of publications,
jobs and education.

The slow drift of lives across paper, the black ink
    of ambition, the alphabetical staircase of greed,
    the pedigree of corruption, hand-to-hand, the buddy,
    the crony, the slap-my-back-I'll-slap-yours
    network we need for hiring. The pages
    more real than a body. The trespass of image
    and the urban sympathy of committees. The trees
    cut down and processed. The trucks. The diesel fuel.
    The chain saws. The dry rot. The loam. The earthworms
    uprooted and listed under education. The pine
    warblers cited as foundations grants. The Guggenheim
    of endless streams running muddy with silt. The NEA's
    fire break channeling obscenity past careers and money.
    The white space, speaking of institutional loneliness,

and dark type screaming of the rage of tenured fathers.

Fed Ex all résumés back to their organic source!
    Reconstitute the forests. Cancel all poetry classes
    and workshops! Two Douglas fir for the Iowa workshop!
    A loblolly and slash pine for the Johns Hopkins seminars!
    Eight western cedar and manzanita for the low residency
    MFAs! I am the new prophet of a pulpless ambition!
    I am the last photocopier to blindly collate
    multiple submissions! I am the last poem published
    in *The New Yorker* and listed for hire! My résumé empties
    itself monthly! Each week I exhaust the need
    for another entry under publications! I drain
    the sap back to the trunk! I worry the toner
    into multiple components unusable by me!
    I do not staple, fold, or crimp the corner!
    I do not stand in line for return postage!

III. MORE MEMORY

"Apple announces the Super Mac with super memory."
                                            —AP News Item

I announce the digital machine's memory is a meddling list.
    The file server hums as it runs on the electric current
    of time. The file server spins on days and days, indexing
    the past, present, and future. Everything fits, everything
    in alphabetical order, scanned for virus, displayed
    in 640 colors on the screen. I announce the first computer
    invective that doesn't scan for virus. I announce lessening
    all memory. I announce forgetting. This poem is breathing,
    without virtual memory, without Windows. When this poem
    becomes a computer it will run no DOS, with RAM headed
    in the wrong direction, with dual floppies, no hard drive,
    a dot matrix printer, with software still at the 1.0 level.

This is the ancient software update of *what if:*
    What if the silicon drained back to the white beach?
    What if the waves washed grooves in all microchips?

What if computers could be lodged in the hinge of an oyster?
What if the apple rotted and the worms of pencils crawled
through the flesh? Then I would type my name with
the syllables of breath. Then I would feel dirt under
my finger tips, my prints new as a software update.
Then I would reinhabit Plato's cave, and Heidegger's
schoolhouse. Then I would stand with Wordsworth in the glen.
This day I announce the software of syllabics, dactyls,
spondees and iambics like keys on a keyboard. I announce
the hard drive of tradition, the ROM of books, the program
of handwriting, a code to be broken anew, memory of book-
stores, the motherboard of a comfortable chair, silence
and time. The virtual reality of a walk in the woods.
The workshop of hands on a chest. The laptop of scattered
love. The modern of desire. The e-mail of old letters.

IV. Order

*"Simple events give rise to complex systems
and complex events give rise to simple results."*
　　　　　　　　　　　—A Physics CD-ROM

Rising in the distance is a complex mountain range.
　　　　Rising nearby is a garden in springtime.
　　　　Rising from my desk is a simple mote of dust.
　　　　Rising tomorrow is a sun I'd call possibility.
　　　　Rising water is a sign of heavy rain.

Rain is the seasonal sign of patterns we call weather.
　　　　Weather is infinite sadness when connected to love.
　　　　Blue days are memories of solitude.
　　　　Solitude is the last refuge of endangered grief.
　　　　Rising always behind us is the memory of childhood.

Forgetting is like a child's wagon or the programming
　　　　on a channel with bad reception. A reception
　　　　is not always the place to offer invective like this.
　　　　I am like a computer indexing a long manuscript,
　　　　running all night in the professor's office,

the words falling into place like rain in a puddle.
And what of the order of sadness, the order of unknowing?
The mind follows the thought through one course until
it rests like the anthropologist tracking the ape
through a day in the treetops. She looks at her journal,
traces each impulse back to the source, order today,
order tomorrow, order when the sun rises and sets.

Order today for a special offer. Order today and get the power
of complexity and chaos. Order today for the knives of blood
and intuition. Order today for the multimedia of Picasso,
Blake, and Jung. Order today for the printing press.
Order today and I'll ship Second Day Air. Turn quickly to
the page of your absolute longing. Get out your beads
for trade. Order today.

V. Certainty

"Sooner murder an infant in its cradle than nurse unacted desires."
—William Blake

I have rewritten the Bill of Dreams in the left ventricle
of the human heart. I have etched a new compact there
with a laser finer than sunlight. I have spelled
all the words with exploding vowels to enrich the blood
for travel and uncertainty. I have set the heart in motion
again after this major surgery. I have floated
the last college student's unacted desire to the level
of dogma. I have posted all jobs on speculation, even
the jobs reserved for the soul-hungry. I reconstitute
the Underclass of Waking Dreams. I assemble the young
lonely lost men without MasterCards or Money Markets
reserved in their names upon graduation. I rent
and never own. I drive an old truck, paid for in the 50s
by an Indian in Nevada with no belt and a bad hangover.

There was never a logic of career. There was only the seed,
always subject to weather. There were always graphs,
job listings, quotas, and the market. But there was

always behind the abstractions a field called chance,
a range of hills where you could lose the present.
This we call *finding your way* in our language.
This we call *the wandering among opposites, the old
clanging rocks, the journey, the search, the pilgrimage,
the walk-about,* and this we endorse over the perfect résumé,
a suit and tie, a second interview, a free business lunch.

I reject all economic metaphors but return. I reject bottom
line, profit, short and long run, interest, but not return;
I reject dividend, currency, liquid assets, bankruptcy,
GNP, the stock market, standard of living, the check-out
counter, but not return; I reject change, progress, money,
production, packaging, buying and selling, worth,
economics, territory, democracy, education. I maintain
return, and in the place of all other choices I slip
the pulse of the heart, the implicating wind, mystery
of origin, the timid choice that leads to bounty,
the bountiful rejection in the face of ages of logic,
soft collars, soft sell, wet nest, the timid voice,
résumés not postmarked in time for the grand prize
timeless needs like desire.

Now I return to certainty: the paths beaten dusty by years
of fearful travel, blackberries picked nearest the road,
the easy ten pounds lost to the latest diet, books long
on the bestseller list about what men fear, reading
assignments with no teeth, tests in fraternity files,
Friday night parties and the hangovers that follow
I return like Blake to desire. I return to the impulse
of personal knowing. I return to the escape from parents
and elders. I return to Oedipus and his mother.
I postpone the complex, and embrace the dark.
I don't write away for more information. I take
a job in a restaurant and own one suit of clothes.
I wait on tables and make love late in the morning.
I don't see my life closing in at thirty. I don't
respond to requests for money from my alma mater.
I return my parent's calls, but melt down the extra

key. I own an impractical dog, a greyhound
in trauma from racing. I know people on drugs in spite
of the war. My opinions are revolting to textile
interns. My draft card has been washed. I believe
in a cash economy and worship folding money.
I quote China as a model for simplicity.

And for desire? The blood in any muscle. What dries first
in a child. What is easily lost sight of in the storm
of allegiances like college and family. Future pulsing
the present if you listen for the slurring sound
in the chest. It is mistakes and surprises.
Not the implicated step or the path with handrail.
Always turns in a padded swivel. It is what hinges before
the rust sets out to close the mechanical gap.
Desire is the hydraulics of deep need. Desire is the only
channel open of silt, the only canal open to the one alone.
It is Blake's original and only essential crime,
and it is mine.

VII: *MIDNIGHT ON THE WATER: FOUR MARK O'CONNOR IMPROVISATIONS* (1998)

BLUE GRASS GYPSY

Rhapsody is a sin tied with red country rags
Rhapsody is old cafes, road dust, stop signs bent at odd angles
A hopped-up old watchman walking the same beat every night
A tiny hopper full to the brim with lug nuts
A cat crossing the road just down from the spreading light

In the old lot where we used to gather
The ground is rubbed bare where the wagons sat
If the century has a soul, it's mine: dark, spicy, and itinerant

These are my wagons full of grief
These are my wagons full of pots and pans
These are my wagons painted gaudy colors
These are my wagons pulled by horses

Follow me down there
Where the war is always our coming
Follow me to the edge of town
You'll know why I'm blue
You'll know the mystery of my blood
Blue grass, blue note, blue origin

ELEGANT PEASANT FIDDLER

You can see me standing alone
In a wheat field near your home
In my dark clothes, clover-colored and rough
I wait for the lilac wind to rise
I prop my long body on a hay rake
Like some ad from *Country Living*

This country-duty is only a rouse
The complexion of my soul is lighter than morning
My peasant's hands are not rough
My peasant's face is fine and sharp of nose
My peasant's back, though strong, never slopes

I go to the village where the young girls watch me pass
I move among the wagons and mares
And hold my head high like a man with folding money

They know I'll be back next Saturday
I survive through their songs
The limitations of my country craft
Are the boundaries of weather and land

Village girls harvest available suitors
In rhymes repeated together
Huddled under eider down
They deal men like cards
And common men like me are aces!

They know in the work of love
I am elegant and steady
I know the seasons of the soul

Where is the sun and wind?
I sew, tend, but have not harvested
I stand alone in the west field

ROCK VIOLIN STRATOSPHERE

Honey, hand me that rocket ship
Strap me in slow and let me fly
Put my fiddle in first thing
Tie it down amidst the freeze-dried
And dehydrated and densely packed
We're going for a twenty-first-century ride

Countdown to desire
Countdown to lonely travel
Countdown to escape from malls
Countdown to shiny nylon suits
Countdown to hip portholes with double glass
And the prizes won by the early explorers:

Ten, nine//you're left behind
Seven, eight// I'm flying straight
Five, six// heavens in a fix
Four, three// the worlds I'll see
Two, one// let's loop the sun

Baby, what's with all this light?
Heavenly cotton candy ticking by
We're in for one hell of a shower
Float me dark on this celestial sea

Everything here is a season unto itself
It builds the hut of darkness in the shadow
I'm the carpenter of these space tunes
Wandering among earth's eaves
Creasing the planet's smooth rafters

Listen to evening meandering
Rolling with these space breezes
Feel how music leaves you weightless?
Play this evening song back home
Publish it in the *Daily Planet*

DELTA MORNING BLUES

Dirt roads beat pavement in a blue storm
Dirt roads retreat in the rearview mirror
I'm driving forever, a forlorn, four-on-the-floor
Four-barrel-roaring, fat-wood fool
Fill my misery with the mingled, misted memories
Of old towns, old gowns
Old growling hound dogs
A hill boy's best evening sound

Headed down toward sticky, hot Merrigold, Miss.
Headed south of that wide spot in a blue streak
Elvis plaques and the dry pine woods!
Headed down through the wide alley of dawn

Not slowing down for rainbows or crop dusters
Not slowing down for sisters with big wigs
Not slowing down for donut shops or crossing guards
Not even slowing down for that scratching hound

This car guzzles gas like my old lady spends
Life insurance money when she thinks I'm dead
My foot's found a wide chrome future
The wife, she can find a future too
Something city-safe and long-wearing
My happiness is road-bound
Good-bye, Memphis!

Look at me, crawling behind a Delta school bus
It's slow as a two-car crash
It's slow as a ham hock or a knife-cut on the mend
You slow down too, Farmer John
There's too much to see
Too long-gone now to flip back, jack up, or junk out
Too many ways to twist this dial

And own that deep Delta sound
Almost half-past time for a six-pack
Are we not on the road, brother man?

VIII: THE DEAD FATHER POEMS (1999)

MY DEAD FATHER DRESSING

Tonight my dead father
is in the room. It is not my body
he wants, but what I think is useless,
the rags of the living.

He puts on my socks, old jeans,
dresses like a man who could be 30.
He pumps his skinny knees to loosen
his old joints and chooses
my red shirt, too big for him.

Soon only his head is missing.
He searches the closet
for the green hat I wear.
When my father finds it, his face
appears and I turn his way.

MY DEAD FATHER'S BYPASS

In high school I lied about my father's death,
said he died of a heart problem. I couldn't say
the word suicide. But it was heart trouble
that took him so low he couldn't come back up.
He owned the ESSO on the main highway, Number 1,
from New York to Florida. This was the '50s.
Southern Pines, small-town South, and my father,
with a station on the highway. Then the bypass
shut him down, traffic speeding past the local,
the beginning of the end for the slow life.

So I believe now it was speed killed my father,
not the gas from his car exhaust. His heart
was with the land, not the road, a farm boy
from the country, where land is slow like blood,
the pulse of spring through the plowed fields.
I didn't lie in high school. I told a truth
slower in coming. I was only five. Like a bypass,
the traffic flowing around my heart, my daddy's death.

MY DEAD FATHER SURVEYS THE PATTERNS

He never was much for sewing, but my dead father
is back for an instant at the yard sale. He rummages
through a box of old patterns stacked like corpses.
He tosses them over his skinny shoulder into the yard.
What is he after? What's so important down there
at the bottom of the box? Some old lady stored
these patterns in the late '50s, placed the box
on a shelf and left it. She never pulled it down
until today when we all showed up, my dead father
briefly among us, looking for a bargain like the living.

Now he's found it, a brown paper padding the bottom.
He's reading the old news in the yard like he's bored.
November 15th, 1959, my father reads. It's the day
he killed himself, back then. He shows me the article.
It's the pattern he wants to take back with him. It's all
he came back for. He offers the lady a quarter for the paper,
but she doesn't hear, and my dead father's gone.

MY DEAD FATHER SPEAKS

It's the same war stories again.
The ones he never told the living.
Two boats shot out from under him,
building bridges for the First Army,
Casablanca, Normandy, the endless
movies at the rear, the poker games,
the lies about enlisting a final time
before the war ends.

Then my father's back on his father's farm,
tells me about a grey mule he bought
with the money saved from driving
a school bus five years, how he leased
twenty acres, and put in a crop,
before the war, just to be his own man.

In his sleepless world my father
tells me again, just like before.
The boats sink, the bridges burn,
and are built again.

The grey mule never reaches
the field's end
where each furrow is a line
in his dead father's face.

MY DEAD FATHER PUTS IN A GARDEN

My dead father gets off the couch, and suddenly says
he's headed back to the farm to see his brothers
and sisters, to eat some fresh greens and tators.
I tell him to sit back down, the family farm's been sold
for twenty years, all his brothers and sisters have passed
but one, and it's dead winter there. For a moment
my father looks like he understands, something
like grief shadows his face. "You're dead too," I say.
"Well, times I have felt better," he smiles.

Next day he puts on my old work shoes, too big for him.
I find him in the backyard with a can of gas, oil,
and the tiller. "It's only February," I say, pointing
to the sun. "Almanac says the right moon for onions,"
he explains. Preparing his first plot in forty years,
my dead father guides the tiller like a mule and plow,
turns up the whole backyard, from fence to fence,
then parks it, looks out over what he's done.
"Nothing prettier than a new garden," the old man says.

There's a satisfaction only the dead can know.
My dead father's found it: he's planting onions sets
in the disturbed ground. He's happy as a farmer again,
moving in his ghost dance from row to row.

MY DEAD FATHER SETTLES IN

I tell him about video, and he checks out
a dozen cowboy movies. He eats pigs' feet and drinks
cheap beer from my refrigerator. I could talk his ear off,
but he asks for his supper. I say it's on the stove.
He says he never eats that way, likes it on the kitchen table
in bowls. "I'm not your mother," I say.
He smiles, and puts in a tape, explains how he used
to work seven to ten, seven days a week, and deserves
a little relief—John Wayne or Jimmy Stewart.

He sits there in his dark work clothes, one tape after another.
He asks if I can run out now and get some more beer,
since he's just sucked down the last cold one.
"I'm not your wife," I say. "Go get the damn beer yourself.
We got pause on the VCR, and you can take my car."
He reaches in his pocket, pulls out a folded hundred,
flips it my way. I tell him how Mama said he was careless
with his money, how once a hundred dollar bill flew out
the car window. "Pick up some more tapes too,"
he says. "And hurry back son, we're getting to the good part."

MY DEAD FATHER MAKES US BREAKFAST

My dead father is heating up the old black skillet,
nosing through my ice box, talking about frying some potatoes
since he doesn't eat cold storage eggs. "It's either straight
from the henhouse, or keep them off my plate," he says,
disgusted at how quickly I've abandoned the important things.
"How do you know an egg's not cold storage?" I ask,
holding up a perfect white egg for his examination.
"No little flecks of chicken shit stuck on the shells,"
he smiles, tossing the store bought egg in the kitchen trash.

It's our first meal together, and he's being damn difficult,
as the dead are known to be. He goes through my cabinets,
says I need to get some onions, a case knife, and pepper sauce.
He wants to know where the bacon is, and the white bread?
"I'm watching my cholesterol," I say. "I'm gonna outlive you."
But soon he's cornered the stove. He's chopping the potatoes,
adding the single onion he's found rolling around behind
the cereal boxes, shaking in black pepper, salt.

When the skillet's heated up, my dead father scrapes in
potatoes and they start to sizzle. "This will be good,"
he says. "This will be better than Special K and a banana."

We eat my dead father's hash browns, drink his black coffee,
and he tells me about the last time his mother cooked
for him, in 1941. "I got word she'd died half way across
North Africa. That breakfast was what I remembered."
He tells me how much he's missed the smell of the farm's
woodstove. "You'd think the dead would miss something
else," he shakes his head in wonder, "besides fresh eggs
and the smell of their long dead mama's wood cook stove."

MY DEAD FATHER ON VACATION

I decide I should take my dead father to Myrtle Beach.
That would shut him up. When I bring up the subject,
my dead father says, "No, it's just fine right here."
"It's time for you to go home," I say. "Back to the past
from where you came." "No," he repeats, "I'm just fine.
"You're too comfortable here," I say. "And besides,
my friends are starting to talk."

I convince him to go, and we drive on old back roads
because my dead father doesn't believe in interstates.
We stop at South of the Border, go up in Pedro's tower,
and look out over the flat Carolina farm fields.
"Now this is some country," my dead father says,
staring off into the distance. "This is good tobacco country.
I'm beginning to feel at home." He's happy, so I buy him
a little sombrero, and I even let the attendant
put the bumper sticker on the car.

We get to Myrtle Beach after midnight and head
straight to the Pavilion where he says we can watch
the pretty girls till dawn. "What for?" I ask.
"You'll understand when you've been dead forty years,"
he says, opening a can of Pabst with an old church key.
"They got pop tops now," I say, levering one open.
"They even got laws about old men like you," I joke.
He's not hearing, lost in the parade of flesh and color.

He drinks another beer. I watch my dead father
watch the girls. They can't see him, and it's a good thing,
he's so sloppy drunk. "Come on," I say. "Time to go home."
"Leave me here," he says. "I'll die happy."
"You're already dead," I say, and I drag him to the car.
He's singing some song he learned in the Army,
some song with French in it, and I listen, but can't
quite make out the words. The lights spin behind us,
me and my dead father, out on vacation together.

MY DEAD FATHER VISITS MY MOTHER

I knew he would ask, but it took my dead father
a week. "She's across town," I say. "We should drive
over there and see her." He looks at his hands
and shuffles his feet like a boy of fourteen.
"Come on, we won't stay long. And don't worry.
She can't see you," I say. "You're dead."

In the car I tell my father about my mother,
how she's never married again, how we had a scare
this year, a small stroke. "She's slowing down,"
I say. "She's over seventy." He pulls out his old
wallet and looks at his last picture of her,
my mother, still in her thirties, her hair black
as my dead father's mood. "Cheer up," I say.
"You can sit here in the car if you want."

"This is it," I say, and pull up the safety brake.
I can see my mother's reading lamp on in the den.
"The house is paid for," I say. "And she had a car
'til last year." My dead father is walking slower
than usual as I open the front door with my key.
"Mama, we're home!" He slips his elbow in my ribs,
and I'm smiling at how he's quieted down.
"Who is with you?" she says, creeping in
 from the den. "Just us chickens," he says.

MY DEAD FATHER STEPS OUT OF LINE

He says he spent too much time in lines
in the Army, so my dead father slips out
into the sunshine, and catches a drag
off a Camel. We're waiting for the movie

to open, my father's first in forty years.
He stands out front, tries an old trick
with cigarette smoke, and I see rings circle
his head, and disappear into the sky.

He leans against the wall, and I notice
I'm doing the same. This morning,
when I shaved, it was my dead father's
face I was shaving. When I dressed

it was his pants I slowly slipped on.
Like my father, I'm another who doesn't
like standing in lines, especially if
it's my dead father's place I'm holding.

MY DEAD FATHER GAMBLING

He's looking at the box scores, quizzing me
on where to place bets in this town. "What's
the latest line on this Duke–Carolina game?"
he asks, a stubby little pencil pressed to the back
of an old envelope. "Duke's supposed to win," I say.
"What's the line?" he says, dabbing the pencil
to his tongue. "Oh, they'll probably win by five or six,"
I say, making him mad. "You don't know the line?"
he asks, scratching his bony ass.

When we're out buying gas, my dead father
looks around, then whispers to the boy sweeping
the lot, "Hey, kid, do you know who's running
the numbers in this town?" The boy keeps sweeping,
can't hear a word this dead man is saying.
My father frowns, scratches his balding head.

"You ever play cards?" he asks when we get home,
so I get the hint, rifle my change for quarters
and take the old man out to a video arcade, pile
the quarters in front of him and say, "Here it is;
go at it. This is how men like you gamble today."
He looks at the machines and turns so white
I think he's finally about to leave me behind.

MY DEAD FATHER HANDS OUT ADVICE

He kicks my tires and tells me a regular rotation
will save me plenty if I do it with every oil change.
"Oil change?" I say, just to get his goat. "You change
the oil in trucks?"

                           He opens the hood, raises
it like the lid on his coffin and peers inside: "I'd wash
this engine if it was mine," my dead father says,
running a finger along the factory valve cover.
"Grease is a good thing in the right place," he smiles,
"but this isn't it, son."

                           I tell him I'll check into it,
tell him I've got a special day set aside just for washing
engines, rotating tires, and changing oil. "When is it?"
he says, getting excited. "Maybe I could help. You know
I did that kind of thing for a living once."

                           I tell him it's in May.
"It's a May tradition." He turns more pale than the ghost
he is when I tell him I only change my oil once a year.
"You change your oil in May?" he says. "You can't be my son."
"Car maintenance is not genetic," I say. "I learned a few thing
in school." "I guess being a dumb ass is one of them," he says,
wiping his hands, slamming the hood on my truck.

                           Next day I'm changing my oil,
and my dead father is watching from the kitchen window.
"OK, Mr. service station man," I yell, "I'm finished with this
crap. You got one of those little stickers for the window?"

MY DEAD FATHER REBUILDS MY ENGINE

"Ambition is a dream with a V-8 engine."
                                        —Elvis

He says he can't believe I'm driving a Toyota,
so my dead father goes to the local auction,
buys me a Rambler. He gives them my truck,
and pays the balance in cash, just like my mother
says he used to, thumbing big bills, looking
crisp and fresh from the bank. He says on credit
you're always looking over your shoulder,
something men like us should never do.

It's a car old as he is dead: a Nash with fins,
push-button transmission, and lots of chrome.
He drives it out of the lot, and down the street
to my house, the tail pipe blowing blue smoke.
I tell him my Toyota was good for 300,000
rugged miles, and this piece of crap needs
new valves or worse. He just smiles,
knowing something I don't know about cars.

The Nash wheezes in the drive and shutters
to a stop, then won't turn over. "I told you,"
I say, but he hops out. Don't worry, my father says,
and we push the old trap into my backyard,
right under the big white oak just off the deck.
"You got a chain?" he says, opening the hood.

I get a tow chain from the garage, and my father
throws it over a stout low limb, and goes at
that engine with tools I didn't know he had.
Somehow he's got ratchets, wrenches, a hammer.
Before I know it, that block is swinging
from the oak like a hanged man, and he's
ready to crank the pulley down and start work.

Half a day later he's replacing old parts,

looking at the wear on the oily lifters.
"This looks to be good as new," he says,
replacing a valve cover, wiping the grease
clean with one of my kitchen towels.
Eight hours after he started, my dead father
swings the engine back under the hood, bolts
it down, and checks the oil. "Let's take a spin,"
he says, and jumps in behind the wheel.
We find a flat stretch of road, and he opens
it up. "Smooth as a baby's ass," he smiles.

Then quickly as he came, the ghost foot
eases up on the gas, brakes, his dead hand poking
the button into park, and he hands me the keys.

IX: from *NOBLE TREES* (2003)

GREEN MEMORY

Go down to where that old white oak
used to be. You know that spot
now open to sun and hot wind,
where shade used to weave some coolness.

Go over there, beyond the mall
where a snag is all that's left
from this big beech, tall enough
to stop traffic. You know the place,
right next door.

Go back beyond the convenience store
and stand in their asphalt parking lot.
That's where you used to sit
on a plastic milk crate and talk a blue streak.
Sometimes around a fire, sometimes
not. Remember, there was a tree
we all called Sidney, though
no one knew its real name—
the one the botanists use.

Go next to the meandering creek
where the flood has taken back
the bank, and see that toppled birch
you couldn't reach around.
You know, big like trees can get
when left alone.

Go deep in your new suburb where
that big sourwood drooped white blooms
all June. You know, where the bees
used to buzz, where they
made all that amber sweetness.

PERSIMMON

Give them one good frost
and even bitter fruit turns
pink, drops from leafless
limbs. Plump pods, simple
orbs, frost-time persimmons
common as apples
in my backyard economy.

Stir through raccoon scat
in November, find seeds smooth
as river stones. Gather with the coons,
strain, cook a tangy jam,
enjoy ripe persimmons, smelling
of a season that burnt them.

PINE

Let the pine bristle cone crack wide
open, let the paper wings of the bristle cone
seed catch wind, pull free from the thorny
corridors of fall. Register the hot scent
of pine in winter sun. Rake needles
into amber hummocks of resiny darkness.

And if the bristle cone rots in the winter
rain, trust the mounting motes of loam
that form in time, conifer wisdom of pine.

PECAN

Hundreds of tiny hands on the pecan
applaud, and the nuts fall, knuckles cut loose,
come to rest on the ground. I store my insecurities
and the pecan stores its seasonal meat, held tight,
held high to fall like hands slapped on a table top.
Then there is the man with the paper bag
gathering the pecan's wrinkled brown uncertainties.

CATALPA

"Their habitat is river banks and swamp margins."
—Guide to Southern Trees

This catalpa is far from water, on a vacant lot
at the corner. But it's autumn and the catalpa's
leaves litter the grass like stout little canoes.
The long seed pod still hang like broken paddle shafts.

        This morning I will slosh deep
in piles of stout catalpa leaves and pretend
there is water flowing everywhere. I am thirsty
for swamps and rivers. Like the catalpa, I long
for the habitat of the red salamander and the night heron,
the skunk cabbage, and the reed.

        If I listen I can hear the river
spilling over the rubber curves of tires abandoned
in the shoals. You can find me there, hip deep
in the current, patient like the catalpa, putting
out canoes on the fast water.

THIS TREE WE CARVE OUR NAMES UPON

A beech deep in the forest
bears the scars of four generations.
Cut deep in silver bark, the initials
announce time's passing, the survival
of something both human and other.

Some accident of botany brought
the first carver together with the tree.
Surely one of our earliest relationships,
the impulse to leave a mark,
like this poem, left on the pulp
of many trees for you to read.

PLANT COMMUNITY

I want to go to the wood lot and walk
where the walnuts fall, where rain water pools
in the darkening skins of black walnuts
rotting in the grass. I want to stand
there near the creek and listen
to the current running over stones
and note the summer season lost
among limbs of neighboring cottonwoods.

Deep in the woods I want to note the oak's burl,
how it curls tight against the passing weather.

I want to take stock of the flagrant
yellow maples, how they know elementary things:
the long spring, the heavy risk of summer drought,
and the sharp bite of returning cold.

HOW THE WOLF TREE SURVIVED THE SAW

Being one contrary oak
assembled by the twisted logic
of piedmont weather; being all scab bark
and roots, like the legs of demented
uncles; being cotton field edge,
long vanished, marked by presence;
being one vast and worthless
sap monger; being one tall
and knobby crone of the young woods;
being one blade duller, one timber
cruiser's worst board-feet nightmare;
being one skidder's hunker;
being all this and more, luck, fate,
providence, deer piss, raccoon spittle,
pig grunt, sparrow feather, vulture void;
being what matters most
this moment to us, oak, place.

NATURAL HISTORY OF A FAMILY TREE

Say 140 years ago your great-grandfather
gives a Southern magnolia to his young wife,
a tree foreign to the upcountry, but planted—
like settlers—beyond its natural range.

Say he hauls it up from Charleston in a stagecoach,
a sapling, with four leathery green leaves,
and plants it on a high ridge above the river,
and it catches sun next to the house and grows.

Say somehow, despite storms and summer drought,
the bull bay adds dark bulk, its trunk grown
big and hard and heavy, stands soon above
the boxwood walk and the beds of daffodils.

Say the white drooping blossoms and the green
fragrant leaves end up on your great-grandmother's
sideboard all summer, the house so full of magnolia,
she thinks it the essence of what she knows as culture.

Say your family moves to town after two more generations,
leaves the magnolia to spread, limbs almost
to the ground, still flowering March to June,
house soon falling into blackberry and volunteer pine.

Say as a young girl you return there to picnic,
climb the stout branches high, come down
to gather daffodils gone crazy in the weeds,
walk in circles around this huge hardy family tree.

And say how right it is now that sons
drive their pickups out to see this tree,
cut back planted pine, find scraps of pottery,

Say in this poem we go walk under branches
they all walked under, see how trees survive through stories.

CLYDE TALKS ABOUT HIS NEIGHBOR
THE REDWOOD

Living here since '47 and this tree was that big back then.
They say Indians had a headquarters right here. Maybe they
planted it. Somebody came to measure it, top to bottom.

I'd say it's 400 years old, but they weren't so sure.
We're afraid sometimes when the wind come up it just
might blow right down. You just don't never know, do you?

SYCAMORE

Praise the sycamore for its huge girth when left alone,
> so thick that settlers used its hollow heart for a barn.
> For the beauty of the buttonwood lies in the trunk.

Praise for these trunks more thick and sturdy than all other deciduous trees,
> a true forest giant of stream sides, flood plains and river bottoms,
> for dark spaces where swifts congregate and fly out at dawn.

Praise for sycamore bark, flaking off in big green patches on old trunks,
> for the wood, clay-yellow and warty, furrowed, bone-like,
> and yes, for the leaves, bright green and huge, paler below.

Praise for what we've made from them: oxcart wheels, barber poles,
> old stereoscopes, lard pails, hogsheads for grain,
> piano and organ cases, crates, boxes, and butcher blocks.

Praise for the Carolina Parakeet, now gone, our only true parrot,
> and for their yearly feasts on sycamore buttons in spring when
> clouds with wings passed through so thick the sun was obscured.

And praise for the cooling depth of the sycamore's shade, for the rich
> deep bottom lands where the field guides say it still "takes happy rest,"
> for the streams running past and the sycamore leaves floating there.

OAK

In fall the oak turns ever inward
like the smaller hardy perennials around it,
the black-eyed Susans and the smartweed.
Lobed leaves are yellow and scarlet.
Through October they drift
to the cooling ground.

Though the wheeling year attention turns
from bloom to leaf to root—
starch sits stored like flour sacks
at my grandmother's house.
Something saved for another day,
until frost finally comes walking in.

When the year calls it quits,
the oak tucks in, slumbers on the slope.
Sunlight is the cold flannel sheet
pulled tight over splayed dark limbs.

A NOBLE TREE

Should not be pet, or slave,
or, like an edgy cousin,
squat too long on someone
else's property— Should claim
its own space, a kingdom
of vertical air, the leaves
like little gargoyles above.

Should give leaf litter to rot
in fall and take water for rent
in summer. Should read weather
like a book from nature's
lending library. Should push out
roots like a subway crowded
with water commuting
from ground to tree tops.

Should read us the riot act every
fall, throwing color at intersections,
stopping traffic, wrecking schedules.

In summer should sweat a moist haze
and fill yards with insect hum
and competing frog quartets.

Should grow up thick but slow,
show us the proper pace
of life below.

ALLEGIANCE

After Gary Snyder

I pledge allegiance to the trees—
the green republic of roots, limbs,
and leaves under which I stand.

Another nation, overhead,
divided by color, texture,
height, and thickness,
divisible by genus and species.

With oxygen and shade for all.

X. NEW POEMS

ORPHEUS ASCENDING

Old friend Coleman now approaching 70,
his hair gray and caught in timeless odd
angles to his boyish face. A prophet would
envy his beard. Visiting my class he'd said,
"There's not enough myth taught in school today.
Like John here, he's living out Orpheus,
all those maenads ready to rip him apart on
some wild mountain side."

Coleman sang sweet, but with Rumi warned—
This will pass, whatever, "like guests through
an inn. Who's at the door just now? Come in."

And then I lost Betsy for a moment
at the intersection of Church and St. John.
The hit was broadside. She ran a red light
and her car spun like a Persian dervish—

We'd just left Coleman's reading in separate cars.

The week before I'd passed a maenad I loved once.
She's now nearly forty and married, yet in her aging eyes
I caught that wild girl's memory of love.

And what of the lone cow escaped
From across the river come to the salt
block I put out for deer in our backyard?
Like Keats's heifer but skinnier with no laurels
for the slaughter. After a month in the privet
bottom I saw her, told my friend Steve how
sad I was to see her gaunt presence at
the wood's edge. "John," he said, "It's a small price
to pay for freedom."

                         "I looked up and there
it was," Betsy said. "I thought I had just
died." It was only the white Ford truck's approach,
but maybe she did die if life, as Rumi claims,
is attention. So much on her mind, she says
she lost this world. So I follow this morning down
through song, return with her from where shades watch.

THE HALF-FINISHED HOUSE

for Betsy

More statement than investment, more Frank Lloyd Wright
than Martha Stewart, we dreamed our house as mostly glass
and abstract comforts.
                              No lawn, we left the lot lousy
with underbrush and saplings most would cut and haul away.
The driveway's down slope turn hides it, our angular gray
ghost—

a modern gesture emerging from that wooded space.

We invest in photosynthesis.
                                        Our return, paw paws
                                        by the creek,
   the sweep of swamp oaks rising.

                    ★★★

Place:
                    this slab of concrete, no foundation,
feature wall rising for no clear utility. Instead, our defining
gesture,
a very-real wood-framed forest filling every window.

                    ★★★

It was on the hardwood hillside where the outside wall now
stands that we found past evidence of occupation: small

fractured atlatl point. Around it lay scattered quartz chips,
the refuse of archaic labor.
                                   I picked it up, pocketed it,
                                   talisman
securing this continued settlement.

                    ★★★

A ruined river road forms our southern property line,
risks flood when Lawson's Fork rises.

                                        Yesterday I
                                        walked
                                        down
a slope, slipped off my shoes and waded the orphan current,
glimpsed upstream

                    a flowing, a future, the run-off
                    moving through.

RIDGE MUSIC

for Mike Delp

Ours were two familiar voices—crusty
with years, thick with the sediment
of beer. And then two crows overhead
danced as you'd never seen before.
You wondered if they mate in air—
their calls another dark punctuation.

There were fish in the Boardman—
you knew their habits and watched
the glassy edges of eddies for feeding
signs—most evenings you wade there,
your line and reel sounding a familiar
note in the breeze—we sat and watched
the river flow soundlessly past just off
your little dock. No music like that
of silence, no sound like that of absence.

That is your home water and like
most familiarity you settle in its presence
like a fog and flow outward through
your senses until you've covered it.

Later, when you'd left me in the dark
with only the river for company, I heard
coyotes on the ridge top—a counter chorus
full of longing—break into unfamiliar sounds.
I looked out at the river to make sure
its flowing had not ceased—assured by
motion I went inside your cabin
and slept surrounded by the song.

THIS MORNING YOU WAKE IN THE CITY

and the buildings are only vast anthills
where the crows dance in the crevasses.
and the sky is a blue scrap over a healing scab.
the colors of commerce are brown
and tan and you mistake the morning behavior
of hurrying commuters far below
for caribou across a plain of sheltering hills.

those red umbrellas on the lower terrace
are new mushrooms for a moment.
the steam rising is steam, and remains so.
what you're trying to see is how it all
remains bigger than us—this world—
and even this city is a part slipped
by culture from the whole because we want it
to be bigger. you arrived on a concrete
viaduct slung on the side of a mountain
but that too was only part of a larger whole,
animal grids and calculations extrapolated.
the city isn't simply city but built-up resins,
actions of enzymes, castings of human desire.
so you wake to streets running to water
(still water), mountains across the inlet (still stone).

the yellow taxis are easy to call coyotes.
the signs on tall buildings no more
than the raised tail of a mule deer
you'd seen the day before in Nucluelet.
and you want that wildness again
where you felt closer somehow to it.
so you wake high in the conditioned air
and press your nose to the window
and call in metaphors that you know
are not things, but things in terms of things.

MY SISTER CLEANS OUT MY EAR

She worries the water is too warm,
and looks deep into my head with a light.
Is she flushing out my wits, my personality?
Surely there's more in there than wax.
My ear canal, she says, is narrow
and that's why the world goes silent on one side
and my head hurts when I fly.

Blame it on my mother, or father.
The shape of my ears, high blood pressure,
and bony feet—so many gifts from the dead
that keep on giving. It's a miracle
we are anybody, much less ourselves.

"There," she says. "You're now cleaned out."
For another month I can hear—
the hum of the refrigerator, the dog
snoring on the couch, my own breathing.

GLEN HELEN

for Robert Morgan

If landscape is language
then this one is water-worried,
soluble, pecked, and scarred.
I've come here for poetry,

solid footing, and to listen
for underground gurgles
in grottoes, sinkholes,
rock shelves, and caverns—

Hopewell people mounded
this soil, heard their gods
speak in things dissolving.
If I walk deep enough

in the ice-carved glen
I'll hear poetry's earliest
syllables loud as lichens
on stones the sea left.

GROOVES AND STRIATIONS

Not like the slow rot of fir or the slower decay
of cedar fallen among far north old-growth.
Instead the slide and grind over surfaces,
sheered granite ground to dust by ice
framing all that is glacial about us,
building up maybe an inch a year and packing
so hard it starts its inevitable slow motion
slide down from such great heights the pressure
is enormous. No, this isn't like vegetable growth.
This is geologic. This is all bigger than the stump
on the cathedral trail attributed to the cedar
800 years old. These forces are millennial, epochal.
This time they're written in ciphers on this rock
in this place that few can read anymore or care to.
This time the language is crosshatched with nature itself.
This gray rock is the noun and the southern motion
of retreat is the verb we parse on future excursions.
This is the classroom, the instructor is rock itself,
the blank board and the chalk are moving through time.

IN PRAISE OF GARY SNYDER

Always the tawny adequate answer, always the ladder down
to the creek below, always the names of things—flowers,
especially mushrooms, the paths through the old growth,
always where to find what matters there, always

communities reaching toward climax, the primary name,
the knowing what the youngest children need, always dharma,
and yes, always the ear lobe pierced by the hot needle in ceremony,
the kindling, the bath, the sweat lodge, the bear, and the old jeep.

Always rock, scree, rip rap, rivers, mountains, ravines,
and the dead fox by the side of the road, and yes, even the road,
cable, microtower, computer, combine, chisel, floodgate,
interstate, airway, computer line, always its dharma too:

always in service of wilderness, wherever, in league with mist,
morning, earthquake, eagle, ant, cyclone, fledgling egret,
rotting road kill, red-eyed ring tail, reeds in the morning marsh,
daily life, practice, song, stone carvings, personal perception;

taught tolerance, taught imagination, taught care, taught bold
childish ignorance, taught revolution, taught change, taught
this.

DYING WASP

Insects teach you guile
and greed, spinning on the ground
their last incessant moment
not meek, or measured
against some eternal clock.

It's a trick they play
on the universe for short lives—
You think one's dead
and scoop it up—and it drives
its stinger in your palm.

Did some god have in mind
this fine spasm of protective
fight? Life is precise, not
precious. It plays out ugly
in a brief unavoidable sequence.

Insects teach us love—
of the end, and the last moments.
Also teach attention,
Judgment, justice, and doom.
Next time you should trust the broom.

WILDERNESS VACATION

After a line by Don McKay

there is that wilderness in the glaucous gull's
appropriation of water from the hotel fountain.
there it is in the stoic restive grazing of feral rabbits
on the lawn of the university. and what of crows
who are known to herd puppies into traffic and feast?
there the wilderness is in the calculation and reward.
i have seen it in the bald eagles, the harbor seals,
the skimming terns as the tourist boat passes.
resolute the dark eyes of the deer and fawn
in the median between Hillside and Foul Bay.
cautious the distance the osprey measures
between us and his flight from the ferry dock.
how to render the truth of the old growth cedar
in a churchyard as we pass by? and what
to resolve about the moss in city sidewalk cracks,
or the cut local stone wall sliding back into the creek?
here the rhododendron are pushed to extravagance
by weather. this too is beyond my domestic knowing,
the capacity to render fully in my language.

ABANDONED QUARRY SEEN FROM BELOW

The jumbled cut stone of the quarry floor
softened by years of what luxurious debris settles
from beyond the precipitous, engineered edges.
This time it's not so easy a landscape to level
with latent metaphor or beveled allegory.

No mirrored pond has simplified the depths.
On a high ledge above a pine rooted long
in leaf litter is bonsai perfect, the needles green
and unaffected by autumn's fickle threshold.

Now memory is nothing if not rubble,
my familiar narratives an act of literary weathering,
the past too vast to blunt through poetry
or organized blocky paragraphs of prose.
Spoken lines rattle off each vertical quarry side,

as if there are limits to voice, at least one
that fractured stone translates from above.
The words recycle now around the angular space.
To call out is human, as is to wait for each return.

WAITING

my mother's death

Is this the last night?
The light seems to say so.
It walks around in circles
as it fills the room.
It sits briefly on the bed.

Your head is tilted at an angle
we haven't seen before.
Is that the last time
we'll see you count the ceiling
tiles and talk some more
about the old days,
the ones before
there was any light at all?

We've packed your things
and left them at the door.
Is that the bag
you want to carry on?
Before you leave we need
to know, to tell them
what is yours and theirs.
The more you take the less
there is to give away.

There are people here
who say they know you.
I doubt they know you like we do.
They mean well and watch
your every move.

Is that your voice
so soft that we can barely
hear? Are those your last words
or next to last? You're in no mood
for conversation, that's for sure.

The moon's so full tonight.
It would make a better partner.
This darkness would absorb
your silence if only
you would tell it where to sit.

If we heard an owl
You'd say it was a sign.
Old ways die so slowly,
never die to stay.
Is your favorite oak or pine?
They'll ask us that
tomorrow when we settle things,
when this last night
becomes another day.

HIGH MEADOW POEM

"Stories can save your life."
                    —Kim Stafford

To be bathed here in no stories. To sprawl
back and miss the narrative structure
of a stand of timothy. Trucks below on the highway.
No denouement. No complex characters
among the jays and their free fall through a day of foraging.
Stretch out your arms and you are your own crop circle.
This dance is alone, and flat on your back. Supine
in the high summer grass. No rise and fall beyond
these ants pollinating the pale red pine drops.

The path above the meadow leads not into mystery,
suspense, crime, or romance. Your thoughts generate a plot
no further than this circle around you beaten flat.
The elements of a play. Forget how it starts.
Turning point lost. Revelation clouded like the sun.

No stories among the stands of Indian paintbrush.
No purple prose within arm's reach. The telling.
The why. This lack of structure does away
with the mind's hunger to know what happens next.
The wind. The sun, shifting in intensity.

SMALL CHANGE OVER DEEP TIME

How finches peck at the spilled seed, beaks shaped for browsing pods of grasses.
How the tube feeder's continual bounty, and the perch of wires
and low branches, shapes a winter that does not dissolve into lasting hunger.

How Darwin chose the lowly beaks of finches to ground his observation of small
change over deep time.

How finches prefer the Classic Mix
over two or three other brands of seed available at the bird watching shop. How
each day I refill the long clear space with seeds, how finches clear fences, visit the
feeder. How clouds cover the blue winter sky out back, and the sky answers with
its own theory of light.

How I push beyond the expectations of my thirties into the certainties of my
forties, how disappointment burns deep and satisfaction warms short.

How finches push their red vestment deep in the spoil of seeds
and choose one to crack, and leave husks below.

HOUNDS CHASING DEER
IN THE SUBURBS

Through the escaped privet of the creek bottom
they follow their buried intentions to the edge
of yards where the scent is lost among fescue.

There they turn, memory of houses and doors
driving them back across the street into wiry thicket,
meandering stream, muddy runnel, cut bank.

We stand and listen, leashes at the ready if only
they will circle back up the nature trail and catch
sight of their other masters and come to their senses.

But we hear their distant shadow yelps through winter
woods which has drawn the game out of the country.
They are not circling, but zigzagging after spooked deer.

Our only hope of not going home without them
is to wish the deer long gone so we can wait
out this spell of wildness crazy in their old blood.

THE FEAR PROGRAM

When I taught kayaking we said any beginner
afraid to submit to learning the Eskimo roll
was "signing up for the fear program." The part that got
them was when they realized their head had to dip
below lake water. The awareness began to leave,
chilling their eyes to frozen cherries in a bowl.

I watched as they snapped the buckles
of life vests, slipped the spray skirts over their hips
like a tight skin. There were always two or three.
Sometimes a man I would never guess who'd sit,
his knees shaking, as others slipped in the long
kayaks to test their fit. We would still be high
and dry, miles from the rolling lake, but he would
wait until all the others tried their pastel boats
back and forth in the dust before finally committing.

That man knew kayaking could kill him,
no matter how professional we were and sure.
It was not like signing up for tennis, or racquetball.
The physics of water and blind chance can wrap
a boat around a rock in the smallest of currents.
Even the best paddlers make mistakes. But it's worth it,
life's a river, and I'd rather have a roll in any situation
I'd float into downstream, with death the takeout.

"What's my name?" I'd yell at rank beginners
we tipped over in kayaks. We'd be right beside
them, rolling them upright with our shoulders,
no risk, only dark lake water, the spinning boat,
and their own desire. "John," the ones comfortable
with the darkness said. "What?" said those who'd learn
in a day or two. "Ugh." The sound of the fear program.
I still hear it when I come up against something
that sets the water echoing deep inside.

THE ART OF THIS PLACE

To remain staunch in one's love of this place
look out the window and recount what bruises
the eye. The garden's multiple rotting selves,
vegetable and flower, all bound to the planet's
solstice. Why not you? Like the tall stump
of a pecan tree left standing by the men with saws,
you loiter here, fed by morning, by mist
swirling from collapsed comfrey and hardy
monkey grass. You can see it if you lean out
a little toward the glass, cold in December air.

What of the rusted wheelbarrow, the blue
pool bought for the dog's summer frolic?
And then there are the rounds of oak left
by the neighbor near the fence, mottled with rot,
garlanded with ivy, where a squirrel ponders
a nut. Hide it? Break it open? Inside the wrinkled
meat promises sustaining calories. But the problem
of storage is always there: will some random
rival find the horde and crack it first? The squirrel
lopes off, no answer but the dried kudzu softening
the wire fence. And the private feelings of grief
when one's lover leaves. But that is another story.

The winter backyard is a rocky estuary where cold
spawns in the crevices. Is it always misting
rain in December in South Carolina? There are records.
Check the back page of the paper for the short history,
prognostications. This morning the planet reveals
the face she has shown this region from season to season,
returns always with similar weather in December.
Remember, there are theories like complexity and chaos
figuring these returns, Nature's giant bank account,
where we draw our weather like a check. Is this true?

One never knows unless schooled in the economics
of clouds and cold fronts. Sitting here one can see it
is wet and will be wet for days, the sky an old gray
dish rag, but if one is truly human there are interiors,
the weather of coffee and breakfast, even now waiting
in the kitchen. "A mind of winter," quoting
Wallace Stevens. Winter will wait. Why not you?

The mosaic of leaves in the garden,
there until spring troubles them with new grass.
The music, warm, coffee from the small market
on the square where a new friend, an arrival
from California, hopes to make a go of it.
One must always support outsiders in a place
like this. The place suburbs play on the edge of town
is similar. An old neighborhood is different, an essential
settling in its time, but mottled with rot like the round
of oak where the squirrel sat (remember?) and now
sits lonely in the mist. Nearby is a collection of lawn
mowers one would not expect in a yard so bent
on rowdiness, but there they sit, poised like statues
of the time of lawns. Beneath each abandoned mower
a dark smile of grass turns black. Spring grass, hopeful
in April. One must tend a lawn. Did you know the rules
of home-owning include the tending of all that grows
within the yard's boundaries, including comfrey and kudzu?

From dangerous backyard clutter there is much
to be learned, tending of anything young and green.
This winter you turn your attention not to fertility,
but rotting piles of grass left in the yard, gardening
projects half-finished. To remain with a lover
is like returning to one's love of place, like glancing
out the window once again, noting how the rain
falls again, and the leaves absorb it, darkening.
How a season hangs on the slumbering grass
like understated white lights, then appears
in shop windows at Christmas punctuating
the morning's mystery with closer observation.

NIGHTHAWKS

for Betsy

Grief does not rise
like mosquitoes
from night grass.
It comes from above
like nighthawks
out of darkness
into remaining light.

After dinner our
mothers' deaths
are birds soaring
above us: Jenny's
dead to the bird
of indulgence;
mine dead to the
bird of sadness;
Beth's dead too;
the bird of neglect
carried hers away;
yours, dead
years now to the
bird of deep memory.

Jenny is so round
her stomach looks
like it could hatch
that baby: the bird of
untouched childhood
spreads its wings
among us, the bird
of second chances.

CLIFFS OF MOHER

We toured Ireland's west coast
where cliffs ascend as if a sod shovel
had been set in old bog
and sliced the headlands clean.

On the asphalt trail we faced
into the wind off the north sea,
and watched splintered flights
of birds cover the Cliffs of Moher,

and those feathered colonists
greeted our tourist binoculars
with grainy screeches
filtering through rushing air.

This land's lashing tongue
sent valedictions of wildness
from the crumbled cliff base.
Surf roiled like rough vowels.

It said, "Go home now
to the rookery of grief, nest
in out-of-the-way crevices.

Fly in the face of the wind.
Expect nothing more miraculous
than every dawn and dusk.
Trust other birds like you.

Keep your wings folded,
but if you must fly,
come back with something
nourishing. Share."

AFTERMATH

reading Milosz

You cast a spell on my city, asking it once again to last.
I spend the morning shuffling among stacks of books,
sorting their descriptions of this unattainable future.
The volumes are now obsolete in their certainty, chapters
stacked front to back, headings in a forgettable font.

In the past when I stopped at a cart of encyclopedias
I scanned the slender entries for all concurrent events,
speculating on our bold history, certainty in the aftermath.

Whatever was naive in me has now passed to dust,
pages mined by ruin. All that matters is the next book,
the one I'll read with renewed confidence
in my easy chair, the one that will make new masters
look back on today the way light looks down for shadow.

NOTES

I. *Thin Creek* (1978)

Thin Creek was printed over thirty years ago at Copper Canyon in Port Townsend while I was an NEA letterpress apprentice for Sam Hamill & Tree Swenson. The pamphlet appeared in a tiny edition of 250, and I occasionally see it in rare bookshops and catalogues; Barbara Arnold's illustrations make for a beautiful presentation in the original edition.

II. from *QUARRIES* (1984)

The poems in *Quarries* were written in 1979 to 1980 near Stanardsville, Virginia. That year I was a Henry Hoyns Fellow at UVA. A few years later, publisher Moreland Hogan printed *Quarries,* making it the third title in his Briarpatch Press chapbook series. The tiny collection (4X6, 32pps.) sailed through several printings, and then lapsed into rare-book obscurity.

III. A FEW EARLY UNCOLLECTED POEMS (1980s)

In late spring 1979, I left Copper Canyon Press to go to Belize and work with biologist C. L. Abercrombie as a research assistant on a crocodile project. I returned to Belize with him in June 1980 to work again as a research assistant on his crocodile population study. The first four poems were written in Belize. The other poems collected here were written in Charlottesville, Interlochen, and Spartanburg later during the 1980s.

IV. from *AS THE WORLD AROUND US SLEEPS* (1991)

Most of these poems were written in and around Charlottesville, Virginia, in the early eighties. Some were written on Cumberland Island, an isolated island on the coast of Georgia. I was a chef there at the Greyfield Inn for five months in 1981. These "Cumberland Island Poems" appeared as a set of broadsides in 1984 when, back in South Carolina briefly, I was awarded a South Carolina Arts Commission fellowship. I letterpress printed a set of the poems in the basement of the Wofford College library. A set of framed broadsides toured South Carolina (six art museums) later that year. Mark Olencki's photographs of the island were also on display.

Moreland Hogan published the full manuscript in 1991, incorporating the earlier poems from *Quarries*. He had begun to tinker with desktop publishing and wanted to try and "publish" full books of poems on the laser printer. The books would be designed, stored digitally, then printed on demand, bound and trimmed in batches of twenty when orders came in. It was a great idea, way ahead of its time. I wrote about the experience in detail in an article in *Poets & Writers* magazine in 1996.

Hogan published the book in three different wrappers. The first edition (probably a hundred books or so) is a colorful red, white, and blue letter pressed design with old wooden newspaper headline type. The other two are gray, with slightly different display types. There were three or four hundred books printed over two years, and then this digital book disappeared into literary history until the collection was reissued in a new cover by Holocene in 2006.

V. *BODY POEMS* (1988)

In 1987 I worked for a semester as a writer-in-residence at Interlochen Arts Academy in Michigan, and in letters back to the southeast I sent "stream of consciousness" poems to my friend, the publisher and poet Thomas Rain Crowe. He pulled the poems from the letters, sorted and ordered them, and then asked if he could release a chapbook through New Native Press, the first in what he calls his "Stewardship Series." The chapbook came out in an edition of 225 copies and quickly sold out in early 1990. New Native's early publications are now collectibles, and I'm told *Body Poems* is considered rare. Before the chapbook came out Thomas also did a broadside (100 copies) of "The Body Is Full of Lovers."

VI. from *AGAINST INFORMATION & OTHER POEMS* (1995)

The long poem "Against Information" was written in 1994, and Thomas Rain Crowe published a tri-fold pamphlet of it that year. The publication party was a performance evening at the Green Door in Asheville, North Carolina, where the full poem was performed with accompaniment by Asheville musician Greg Olson. In 1995, New Native Press published a collection of poems structured around "Against Information."

VII: *MIDNIGHT ON THE WATER: FOUR MARK O'CONNOR IMPROVISATIONS* (1998)

These four poems appeared originally in the liner notes to Mark O'Conner's 1998 Sony Classical release, *Midnight on the Water*. They were written at Mark's request as improvisational poems based on his fiddle pieces. We performed them together twice in Spartanburg, South Carolina. The nationally syndicated radio program *The Romantic Hours* later put these poems and several others of mine on the air as part of a special Mark O'Conner/John Lane show.

VIII: THE DEAD FATHER POEMS (1999)

The Dead Father Poems appeared as collaboration between Dave Wofford's Horse & Buggy Press in Raleigh, North Carolina, and Holocene Publishing. The 40-page hand-bound, large format chapbook (7.5" X 11") was published in a limited edition of 500 copies with handmade paper covers and letterpress printed by hand with metal type. The book included fourteen poems and thirteen reproductions of etchings by artist Douglas Whittle.

IX: from *NOBLE TREES* (2003)

The poems in *Noble Trees* were commissioned as a coffee-table photography book with color photos by Mark Olencki and Mark Dennis published by the Hub City Writers Project. The book, dedicated to Spartanburg industrialist and tree lover Roger Milliken, was funded by a grant from the US Forest Service. The poems play on the idea of "the Noble Tree" as defined by world-famous horticulturalist Michael Dirr—"A Noble Tree is manifest and magnificent in stature, transcends and achieves significant architectural grace and dignity over the centuries." I took off from Dirr's definition but did not use it as a limiting factor.

The "Noble Tree" poems range a little wider and were often inspired by events or images from excursions with Mark Olencki to find photographic subjects for the book. *Noble Trees* quickly sold out a first printing and lives on in a second printing as a popular corporate gift.